What people are saying about *Dancing Backwards in High Heels*....

"Patricia O'Gorman teaches us how to rely on our resilience so we can gain access to our considerable personal power. This book is a valuable compass to use in navigating through our challenging lives. Every woman needs to read this book."

—DONNA BOUNDY, MSW
Author of *When Money Is a Drug*

"Patricia O'Gorman has been a leading light in the self-help field for years. She has helped pry open m̶ heart is book will help many more."

...Stage II Recovery

"Patricia O'Gorman offers something to every woman who has ever struggled to move forward in her life, her career, and her relationships."

—KAREN CASEY
Author of *Each Day a New Beginning*
and *A Woman's Spirit*

"Patricia O'Gorman shows us what we are made of—far more than we think!"

—JANE MARKS
Author of *We Have a Problem*
and *The Hidden Children: The Secret Survivors of the Holocaust*

"This remarkable book focuses on revealing the natural resilience and inner strength that women possess as their birthright."

—WAYNE KRITSBERG
Author of *The Invisible Wound:
A New Approach to Healing Childhood Sexual Trauma*

Dancing Backwards in High Heels

Dancing Backwards in High Heels

How Women Master the Art of Resilience

Patricia O'Gorman, Ph.D.

 HAZELDEN®

Hazelden Educational Materials
Center City, Minnesota 55012-0176

Library of Congress Cataloging-in-Publication Data
O'Gorman, Patricia A.
    Dancing backwards in high heels : how women master the art of
resilience /Patricia O'Gorman
        p. cm.
    Includes bibliographical references and index.
    ISBN 0-89486-998-1
    1. Women—Psychology. 2. Resilience (Personality trait)
    3. Self-esteem in women. I. Title.
HQ1206.035 1994   94-18598
155.6 33—dc20   CIP

Editor's note

Hazelden Educational Materials offers a variety of information on chemical
dependency and related areas. Our publications do not necessarily represent
Hazelden's programs, nor do they officially speak for any Twelve Step organization.

The names of the people in this book who have shared their experiences
have been changed. This book also includes some stories that are composites
taken from a group of people who have had similar experiences. In the latter
case, any resemblance to specific people or specific situations is accidental.

To the women in my family—my mother, sister, grandmothers, and aunts—who taught me about resilience, and to Sophie Elam, Ruth Sondheimer, Cynthia Levy, and Joanne Dobson, who helped me see this in myself.

CONTENTS

ACKNOWLEDGMENTS

HEARTFELT APPRECIATION TO Barbara S. Brauer, whose skills, vision, humor, and friendship made the writing of this book not only possible but also pleasurable.

Loving gratitude to Robert Ross for his unceasing support and devotion, and to Michael and Jeremy for their sustaining love, pride, and willingness to comprehend, as only the very young can do, their mother's need to write, even when this meant I could not be with them.

Special thanks to Candice Fuhrman, my agent, who believed in this project from the beginning, and whose guidance and tenacity helped make it happen, and to my editor, Rebecca Post, for her enthusiasm and her insistence that this book be as clear as possible.

And I would like to recognize Dr. Steven Wolin, whose pioneering work in resilience helped stimulate me in the formation of these concepts.

I would also like to acknowledge my father, Patrick O'Gorman, for his belief that I could be all that I aspired to; Wayne Kritsberg, who encouraged me to begin this effort; Peter and Sarah Dallas; Lynn MacPhearson; Leslie Boyd; Lisa Dobson; Carl Mindell; Lynn Peseckis; Naureen and Janel Perkins; and my women's breakfast group: Joanne Dobson, Miriam Duhan, Joan Bloomberg, Barbara Nagler, Liz Wilen-Berg, and Rebecca McBride, for their ongoing nurturing and comments on the manuscript.

CHAPTER 1

Women and Resilience: Dancing Backwards in High Heels

esilience? What does resilience have to do with me? I hear this question often from friends and the women I counsel. My answer is always the same: *Everything.*

It is all too common for us women to doubt our abilities, to see nothing extraordinary or powerful about ourselves. Yet if we stop for a moment to consider how much we actually accomplish each day, the many roles we play, and the distances we travel, we may see quite another view of ourselves. This is what our resilience can give us, the ability to align ourselves with our strengths and to recognize our personal power.

The fact is, most of us underestimate the degree of strength and flexibility our lives require on a daily basis. We focus instead on our unfinished tasks and unfulfilled goals. We do not realize how much we ask of ourselves, having done so much and yet expecting ourselves to do more. We need to be reminded of this from time to time, as Governor Ann Richards of Texas (then state treasurer) did in her keynote address to the 1988 Democratic Convention. She pointed out the irony that while Fred Astaire received top billing, "Ginger Rogers did everything that Fred Astaire did. She just did it backwards and in high heels."

1

All women have the potential to master the art of resilience. We all share a special ability to take charge of our lives and find for ourselves the meaning, richness, and purpose we seek. Our inner resilience is the power to know what we need and the strength to act on that knowledge.

Many of us have relied on this inner compass for so long that we are not even aware of it. When we need to make a decision on what is right for us, our resilience is there to guide us. If we permit it, our resilience can inform and shape our actions and responses to allow us to be the person we want to be. All we need to do is listen. This book will show you how; it offers you a comprehensive, practical guide to understanding your own resilience and its role in everyday life.

Discovering Resilience

Resilience is the ability to recognize our personal power, to see ourselves and our lives in new ways. When I think of resilient women, I often think of Angela, a merit scholar from Texas I met at college. I admired her exuberance and her uncanny ability to land on her feet no matter what the situation. She explained that this survival technique was the result of her upbringing in a large family that traveled extensively each summer as fruit pickers.

"We spent five months out of the year following the crops on the Pacific Coast," said Angela. "Believe me, in a family of eight living in a trailer, you've got to be flexible. Moving to a new job, you'd never know what you'd find. It taught us to rely on ourselves, each other, and the other families we met on the runs. We had a real sense of community, something I know a lot of people never find.

"My grandparents came from Oklahoma during the Depression. Like most of the Dust Bowl refugees, they came with dreams and the grit to make them come true. They did what they needed to survive and provide for their families. Fruit picking and other farm work was something they enjoyed; it kept them close to the land and the seasons. It kept the families close together, too."

Angela was the first in her family to go to college, but she regarded this as part of her family's tradition. Angela said, "I was looking for a greener pasture, a way to better my life. Like them, I was ready to work to make that dream come true. I was really just following in their footsteps."

I was intrigued by Angela's stories and her warm humor. I soon realized that while Angela was unusual, she was not unique. Many people have this quality of confidence and inner knowing. Like all of us, they struggle with life's difficulties—setbacks, transitions, loss— but whatever problems they encounter, they refuse to be overwhelmed or beaten down.

As a psychologist, my curiosity was piqued: What was this ability, this inner strength that enables people to weather life's challenges and consistently come out on top? Over the years I've come to identify that quality as resilience. I've also come to see that resilience is a universal trait.

What Is Resilience?

Resilience is a new term for a concept that has evolved slowly over the last few decades, and which is only now beginning to receive widespread attention. In psychological and sociological literature, *resilience* is used to describe people who lead normal, fulfilling lives despite having been subjected to trauma, or who, because of their early home life, are at high risk for developing personal and social problems. The term has been used to describe Holocaust survivors and children growing up in abusive and difficult homes. These people are labeled resilient because they possess the ability to recover from the adversity they have experienced and retain a positive self-image and view of the world.

As a result of such clinical definitions, resilience is frequently thought of as a quality belonging only to those who have survived great hardship. Yet all healthy people are naturally resilient. Just as our body has the resilience to protect itself from disease and heal after injury, so we have psychological resilience. In the body, a certain amount of exposure to disease, such as childhood chicken pox, immunizes us against future illness; we build antibodies and become more resistant. With regular exercise, our bodies become stronger, more flexible and ready to respond to challenge and stress. Likewise, a certain amount of stress strengthens our psychological resilience and increases our ability to handle greater and greater challenges.

Psychological resilience draws on all aspects of the self: emotion, intellect, and spirit. As individuals, we develop our own means of coping with life, our own unique point of view. The exact nature and form of our resilience are as unique as our personality. How we experience our resilience and how it manifests itself depend upon who we are and what we have experienced in our lives.

We all know people who have tackled a major challenge and won against overwhelming odds. The popular play about Anne Sullivan and Helen Keller, for example, is aptly named *The Miracle Worker*. We have heard of the courage many people show in the face of death, disease, or tragedy. We have seen time and time again how whole communities pick up their lives and begin again in the aftermath of catastrophe, such as hurricane, fire, or flood. All of these are testimony to our innate resilience.

Each of us demonstrates resilience in small ways, too: when we reach for the telephone to talk to a supportive friend, when we find the courage to end a destructive relationship or make a new beginning, when we take a deep breath and try again when things don't go as planned. In drawing upon our strengths, we draw on our resilience. We may express it in any number of ways—through our intellectual abilities, creativity, good humor, or sheer tenacity. We each develop our own style and source of strength—whatever allows us to face the challenge and prevail.

Becoming conscious of our strengths makes us stronger. Our resilience increases as we recognize the magnitude of what we have already accomplished, for we come to believe we can do as much and more again. This represents a new, more positive, even dynamic, view of how people can live a successful, satisfying life. It replaces the myopic focus on obstacles and problems by widening the perspective to look past the problems to focus on their solutions.

The Essential Piece

Unfortunately, many people have never consciously discovered their resilience and remain cut off from actively developing this part of themselves. As a therapist and seminar leader specializing in women's issues, I've seen hundreds of women in this situation. They come to counseling or seminars seeking an essential piece that is missing from their lives. They may be women who are raising families and working part time, feeling overwhelmed and understimulated; or successful yet dissatisfied career women who do not have the time or energy for a meaningful relationship in their lives. Many of these women inexplicably find themselves battling a sense of isolation and loneliness that pervades their lives, or trying to match up to standards that seem beyond their ability.

In some cases, these women are facing a difficult transition, such as a divorce, job loss, or new motherhood, and feel unequal to its demands. Others are survivors of childhood trauma and hardship, who at times find their energies so focused on the past or the resultant pain that they have little energy available to meet the challenges of their adult lives.

All these women feel powerless and somehow blame themselves for not being happier, more fulfilled, more at peace with the lives they lead. They often experience a restlessness, a frustration they cannot define. They seek more control over their lives and the means to make the changes they need to bring about a satisfying balance. The essential piece they seek is their resilience.

Everyday Heroism

In working with these women, my goal is to help them understand their own resilient qualities. I help them develop a vocabulary of their unique personal strengths and show them that they already rely upon their resilience and can learn to develop it further.

I help these women acknowledge their extensive accomplishments by asking them to consider the myriad tasks they routinely perform for home and family, employer and friends. Through appreciation for their daily struggles they can begin to see how much they rely on their resilience on a daily basis. When they look at each small task that they handle so expertly, these tasks seem commonplace, manageable, and perhaps of little consequence. But when all of these demands are considered together, they take on a new dimension, an everyday heroism.

The Blueprint

This attention to ourselves and to our countless daily successes, large and small, reveals the tangible benefits of our resilience. We begin to see our resilience as a blueprint, an inner structure around which we can gather and organize our strengths. We can then use this blueprint to make the important changes we need in our lives. When we learn to trust ourselves, we can move forward more confidently, with a new acceptance of who we are.

Tanya, a bright twenty-five-year-old law student, had decided her shyness would be a liability in her career as a lawyer. To overcome her shyness, she insisted on forcing herself into situations that would "snap her out of it." The result was that she was often nervous and uncomfortable, but still shy. The more she struggled to change this, the more ineffectual she felt.

Her discomfort increased as the end of the school year grew near, and job interviews were scheduled. When her schoolwork suffered, she sought counseling.

As we talked about her childhood and adolescence, Tanya told me that she had been happiest during those periods in which she had arranged her life to accommodate her shyness, rather than trying to overcome it. In high school she had had many friends but avoided large gatherings. At college she worked in the school library rather than as a waitress or store clerk.

"What made you choose to go into law?" I asked.

"The challenge of it, the intricacies," Tanya answered. "I enjoy wrestling with facts, their interpretation, and the implications for precedence." As she talked, I noticed how animated Tanya became and how her entire demeanor brightened.

Looking again at her high school and college years, Tanya recognized the wisdom of her earlier choices and saw the benefit of making similar choices as an adult. She realized that her shyness had not kept her from what she wanted in the past and that there was no reason it should keep her from what she wanted now. She began to recognize that her natural aptitude for the law was far more important than her shyness, both to herself and prospective employers.

Like many people, Tanya took for granted the wise choices she had made so easily and naturally earlier in her life. Now, in a new setting, she no longer trusted herself but tried to impose unrealistic expectations she believed she should fulfill. Reminded of her earlier self-understanding, Tanya once again trusted her instincts to make the best decisions.

As she returned to her schoolwork with a new interest in demonstrating her personal strengths, Tanya was amazed at how quickly her shyness became insignificant. She began to take charge of her life and factor her shyness into her decision making. No longer at the mercy of her shyness, Tanya once again excelled at her studies. And when she finished her law degree, Tanya chose to work in the research department of a law firm rather than in litigation.

When we know who we are and hold realistic expectations for ourselves, we can take pride in our assets rather than fighting with ourselves. We stop squandering energy on shoulds and have-tos and begin to accomplish our true goals. When we are assured of our personal strengths, we can more readily accept our liabilities.

Our Own Style

One challenge of adulthood is to recognize our individuality: what makes us the unique person we are. In this, our resilience can serve as a valuable guide. It enables us to examine what qualities are our own and what qualities we have borrowed inappropriately from others.

To accomplish this we need first to become aware of our personal style of resilience so that we can make it more balanced, more consistently present in all areas of our lives, and use it on a daily basis as well as in times of stress and crisis. We can begin by observing the situations in which we claim our power and those in which we yield it.

Before the birth of her twins, Virginia worked part time at a grammar school as the volunteer coordinator for school events. Those she worked with admired her flexibility, good humor, and ability to keep everyone working together. If it needed doing, they all knew they could count on Virginia.

Once her daughters were born, however, Virginia became another person.

"I was exhausted," she explained. "The house was in a perpetual state of chaos, and I couldn't seem to get a handle on any of it. Not that my husband didn't try to help. He watched the kids almost all day Saturday when I did the shopping. But he worked during the week. I told myself it was unfair to ask him to do more when he came home at night. In fact, I made it a point to have the girls washed and fed before he got home. There is nothing worse than coming home to two screaming kids!"

In exploring her predicament, it became clear that Virginia, so competent at work where she easily delegated responsibilities and kept everyone on track, was unable to translate these skills from work to home. Once she became a mother, she put aside her professional flexibility and took on sole responsibility for her home and children. Her model in this, she explained, was her mother; Virginia wanted to be for her husband and daughters all her mother had been for her when she was growing up.

"With three children, my mother always had the house spotless and everything in order," said Virginia. "And she had time for me and my boy talk. That's what a mother should be, I decided. Just like her, I wasn't working. I was home all day. So why, I asked myself, can't I get things done and get on top of it the way she did? Sure, she had the neighbors to call on for some child care, but all our neighbors work. We can't afford a nanny or a maid. I said to myself, I guess I'm stuck.

"When I heard myself say that, I cringed. I'd never been stuck in my life. I refuse to be beaten! That's when I hit on the idea of beginning a mothers' support and play group. It took quite a bit of telephoning and scheduling, but I'm a pro at that. Besides the larger group that meets twice a month, three of us have organized a housework routine: one watches the kids and the other two pair up and clean house.

"This was my salvation. For one thing, I'm not struggling to live up to unattainable standards. I still don't know how my mother managed it, but now I know she's the exception, not the rule. So I can let that hurdle go. Secondly, I like people; friends are important to me. I get more done, not less, when I have a friend to talk to."

When we are true to who we are, our personal strengths and priorities, our own needs and unique gifts, we often find new energy and confidence. We are better able to meet our challenges and overcome them.

Woman to Woman

Resilience is a quality inherent to all human beings, male and female. Yet I have addressed this book specifically to women because they, more than men, are particularly vulnerable to losing touch with their personal power. I believe the particular issues confronted by women in the process of discovering their resilience are different than those experienced by men.

For example, women traditionally have derived strength and identity through their connectedness and relationships with others. They are often other-directed, observant of the people around them, particularly those who share their lives. At the same time, to access their resilience, they must learn to listen to the inner messages and signals of the resilient self. We are most successful in life when we can achieve a balance between these two vital sources of strength: self and other.

Self-expectations and other-directedness can lead many women to assume primary responsibility for the care of others. Madelyn is typical. The eldest daughter in a family with four children, Madelyn was always the strong one in the family. She acted as a second mother to her siblings, and she continued this role into adulthood. When her mother died, Madelyn was there to take charge of her invalid father and settle her mother's affairs—this in addition to her full-time job and family of her own.

"With all that to do, I don't have time to get caught up in feeling sorry for myself," she said.

A year after her mother's death, Madelyn came into therapy to understand why she felt so distanced from her life. She said, "I feel like an impostor, going through the motions. Everything is the same in my life, but somehow it doesn't seem like much. My husband asks me what's wrong, but I can't tell him. I don't know."

Like many women, Madelyn identified strongly with her role as nurturer and family caretaker. She was constantly giving to others at the expense of her own needs. Eventually, women like Madelyn find themselves saying silently, *What about me?* even though they struggle with their guilt about feeling this way. In an effort to still the inner voice that reminds them of their own neediness, they may resort to compulsive spending, overeating, alcohol or other drug abuse, or other self-destructive behaviors.

In therapy Madelyn began to understand that the cost of shutting off her own feelings was greater than the pain generated by allowing herself to acknowledge them. Taking time for herself would not compromise her ability to give to others, but deepen it. She came to understand that to keep giving she needed to receive. She needed to honor her own grief about her mother's death as she had honored the grief of her father and other family members. She deserved to be able to do so.

Madelyn realized that the same skills that allowed her to run her home and nurture her family could also allow her to organize activities to nurture herself. She could get back in touch with her own needs and feel a connection to herself and her life as an individual again.

It is important that women see that the traditionally feminine role of nurturer can indeed give them a source of strength and identity, but if unbalanced, it can rob them of their ability to care for themselves. They can become trapped and overpowered, rather than enhanced and empowered, by their caregiving role.

To own our power means to allow ourselves to derive benefit from who we truly are and what we need. This means to acknowledge our everyday heroic acts and our traditional sources of strength as we practice more consciously and deliberately our own personal strength—our resilience.

Through this new self-awareness a fuller image of ourselves emerges. We discover more power, clarity, and determination to care for ourselves. By accessing our resilience, we can discover the fulfillment that we so deserve. Those who have faced trauma can find healing as they acquire new pride and acceptance, in place of shame and guilt, for the unique survival skills that saw them through. Our resilience is our most powerful tool in our ability not only to survive but to thrive.

The Role of Resilience in Our Lives

To learn of our resilience is to learn to listen inward. Here we find a new acceptance and no longer need to live up to external standards or the "shoulds" dictated to us by others' expectations. Such acceptance fosters our self-esteem. Our outlook becomes more confident and more optimistic. We begin each day feeling we can accomplish what we need. What we don't or can't accomplish becomes less important. We can set realistic goals for the short and the long term and build strategies to reach them, thereby resuming control over our lives through our resilience.

This book's purpose is to teach you to realize your own potential, to know and nurture yourself, and to create and follow your own blueprint to achieve self-fulfillment. As you claim your personal power, you can use it to find more meaning and balance in life.

This is a large undertaking, because it encompasses so many parts of ourselves—past, present, and future. We need to understand the impact of our family on our development as women, including the rules we were given, the interactions we experienced, and the meanings we attached to them. Then we need to look beyond our families to the larger context of society and human history, and the lessons we have learned therein about being a woman.

In our individualistic, competitive society, we are taught more and more to look outside ourselves for recognition, value, and purpose. We are inundated by the popular press and other media with conflicting messages about what we as women should do and be. We may stop listening to ourselves and hear only these outside messages. Unaware of our need to be true to ourselves, we, like Virginia, may struggle fruitlessly to fulfill unrealistic or ill-suited roles and lifestyles, rather than drawing on our own unique strengths and talents. We may judge ourselves against popular role models or struggle against external standards rather than our own inner values.

For this reason, the lessons society has taught us from our earliest years have a direct bearing on the development of our resilience as women. In later chapters we will examine how we are taught to view women in our larger society: what our social institutions teach men and women about themselves and one another, and the conclusions we women draw about our relative worth.

In this book I will show you how to identify your own resilience and how to build it into your daily life to provide nurturing support and guidance on an ongoing basis. You can define your roots as you come to understand more clearly who you are and how your childhood and your family—most importantly your mother, your primary role model—affected and continue to affect your life in both positive and negative ways. I will show you also how to work with your resilience to resolve the long-standing issues that may affect your ability to be who you want to be and live the way you choose, issues that may be keeping you from realizing your potential.

This book will hold up a new mirror in which you can begin to see yourself in new ways. By means of our resilience, we can claim the best of our heritage and lay to rest its painful aspects. We can learn to make choices that take our needs into consideration, and we can learn to plan, to dream, to dare. Our resilience is a powerful transformational tool that allows us to make the most of our experiences, even pain and trauma. This journey promises more confidence, greater self-assurance, and deeper joy.

In knowing our resilience abides within us, we can look ahead more confidently to the future and trust that we have the strength and wisdom to face changes and inevitable losses. We realize we are bigger than our challenges and can learn to celebrate life's seasons and cycles. In doing so, we master the art of resilience.

Do You Use Your Resilience?

Take a moment to ask yourself whether you agree or disagree with the following statements.

- I am able to accomplish the tasks I decide are important.
- I make room in my life for my own needs.
- I love myself.
- I make my own luck.

- I can take care of myself.
- I can choose safe people to be in my life.
- I feel lovable just as I am.
- When I am in love with another I continue to love myself.
- I never feel someone is my "better half."
- I feel competent.
- I can learn from difficult experiences.
- I am motivated from within, instead of reacting to what is outside of me.
- I have an inner optimism.
- I do not make excuses for who I am.
- I am flexible and able to develop new solutions to existing problems.
- I feel pride in myself.

If you agree with all or most of these statements, you probably already use your resilience on a regular basis.

CHAPTER 2

Our Resilient Voice

We may come to know of our resilience in many ways: intuitive reasoning, a spontaneous action that saves the day, an insight that points us in a new direction or validates dimly perceived feelings. We may have relied on our resilience, this "sixth sense," many times and not even have been aware of it. Yet when we become aware of it, we can learn to use its counsel to help us decide what is right for us. Learning to use resilience is a matter of learning to listen.

Several days after her family reunion, Anne told me, "I walked around smiling during my parents' forty-fifth wedding anniversary, but inwardly I was furious—an old, familiar feeling I'd never named before. All these hidden agendas! My mother, sister, and aunts fawning over all the men in the family and then cutting them down as soon as they were out of earshot—even grandma! They boast to one another how they have tricked their husbands into doing things for them, buying them things. They do it all the time. How could I have not noticed it before? What a female tradition!

"This time as they were talking I realized how much I dislike this part of my family. I felt literally ill. I thought it was too much coffee. Now I realize it was just too much duplicity. When I tried to talk about some of the changes going on in our lives, no one wanted to listen. Talk about something real? Something to do with feelings? Never. I am so tired of being invisible," Anne said, "and I am so angry.

"So there I was, caught up in the same trap I get into every time I see my family. I always forget how it works, or I think it will be different. But this time, I stopped to ask, What's going on? I took a little time to step back and get a better perspective. I could see myself playing along with a game I'd never liked. I said to myself, I can't put up with this any more. Then I thought, I don't have to. I can leave!"

Anne told her family she and her husband had to leave early and would have to miss the family brunch the next day. She said, "Maybe I'm learning to protect myself, to establish some limits about how much I can do for my family and how much I need to do for myself. It felt great. Finally, I was standing up for myself and taking care of me!"

Anne had begun to separate from her old patterns and listen to her needs. Realizing her feelings about her family instead of suppressing them, Anne took an important step toward drawing on her resilience to discover options to protect herself and what belongs to her.

This one act led her to establish more realistic and satisfying boundaries. In fact, it was a turning point in her life. "I began to feel that there was more of me," Anne said. "Now I pay attention to the physical clues I get when something is wrong. I'm alert to situations that I need to change, whether it's with my children, on the job, or whatever. I don't put up with as much as I did before, and I'm a lot happier for it."

How We Perceive Our Resilience

There are numerous ways in which we may perceive our resilience. Like Anne, we may actually hear a voice speak to us in seemingly random thoughts. Or we may experience our resilience in the images of dreams or fantasies, as a narrative voice in writing, or as a presence. The first step, then, is to learn how our resilience "speaks" to us and how we can create a dialogue with it.

Sylvia was a participant in a retreat I led. She told me, "As we began to work with the concept of our resilient voice, a part of me was skeptical. But another part of me thought, This is right, this is familiar. It was when I invited this part of me to write a letter that I suddenly knew that I had had conversations with this presence before.

"As a teenager and young adult, I was a journal writer. I would write and write about how I felt about things. Everyday things. Many times it seemed as if there were two voices: after I'd written something, another voice would come in to comment on it. I used to be surprised when that second voice seemed to be a little smarter, as if it had an answer or information I didn't.

"I vividly remember one such dialogue. On my twenty-third birthday I was upset because my husband, Marty, chose to fly to Chicago a day early to attend a professional conference. I was hurt, angry, and feeling pretty unimportant. Even so, I tried to believe it when he told me it was an important opportunity and that he was sorry he had to leave on my birthday. So I wrote in my journal about it. When I got to the part about how I guessed he really was sorry and meant it when he said he loved me, I wrote, 'If he really cared, he would have stayed home on your special day and gone the next day. What about *you* being upset? It was *your* birthday.' "

Two months later, Marty announced that he wanted a divorce. Sylvia said, "I was devastated. I was amazed, too, that while consciously I had chosen not to see it coming, another part of me had. That part saw through to the bigger picture.

"This happened more than once. Throughout my life, this voice said, 'Hey, what about *you?*' This voice was not always good news. I preferred to think that Marty really needed to go early, but somehow I knew that more was going on. I can't always say that the voice was a comfort, but it was always on my side, sometimes more than I was!"

An Inner Presence

Jennifer's discovery of her resilient voice was less direct. She first acknowledged this part of herself in a recovery group for incest survivors.

"Through all my years of counseling and working on the incest," said Jennifer, "I somehow always blamed myself. Not intellectually. I knew enough to say, 'I was only a child. How was a child to know?' But emotionally I just couldn't forgive myself. I couldn't accept that I had not been strong enough to make the incest stop. I kept beating myself up for my innocence, my vulnerability, my stupidity.

"I was sitting in the group, listening to another member share her feelings of shame—feelings that I know so well—when I felt an opening inside. My resilient voice wasn't so much a voice as a presence, like a guardian angel. Somehow I felt full in a place where I had always felt empty. I felt protected, understood, loved, and perhaps most of all, pride for what I had had the courage to endure. This allowed me to *feel* for the first time that the incest *wasn't* my fault. This presence had a special wisdom that I trusted.

"I have this feeling today, like a place within me, a centering. I know my resilience more through feelings than words. I feel as though my vulnerability is surrounded by love. I sense a capacity to love, accept, even nurture myself, that I have never felt before. I feel safe for the first time in my life. I am learning to make an inner home by connecting to my resilient voice."

Jennifer's experience is common among women who have experienced childhood trauma. Their resilience at first is less accessible, more obscured, but still available if they seek it. It can serve to give these women the perspective and self-compassion they need.

Jennifer quickly learned to draw on this inner resource. She said, "Strangely, this part of me never felt new. It always felt familiar, like an old friend I'd just gotten in touch with. I realized that my resilience had always been with me, guiding me, loving me. But when the incest began it was too painful, too confusing to listen to this inner love and wisdom and still do what I was told to do to be a 'good daughter.' So I closed down part of me and lived to survive. Now I can use this part of me to heal."

Through the Unconscious

For many women the first awareness of their resilient voice is through an unusual dream that points a new way, demonstrates new feelings, or clarifies an ongoing problem. Chris told me that she had had a disturbing dream which had awakened her, but without the usual fear that had accompanied such dreams in the past.

"In the dream I am on an old train and have just given birth to a baby. The baby begins to nurse. It is a little painful. I wince but enjoy the moment. I am falling in love with my child. All of a sudden my baby is wrenched from my arms by an older woman. I can't or don't move. The woman is dressed like a gypsy and is leading a band of men and women. They kidnap my child and I never see her again.

"I woke up not afraid, but confused. I kept thinking, *You see, you did have a baby!* when I know I have never had a child. Why didn't I move? In waking life when something like that happens to me I fight back, but in the dream I was so sapped of strength I couldn't move.

"The dream stayed with me. Over the next few weeks, it was just around the edge of my consciousness, waiting for me, and my thoughts drifted there often. Along with this dream came a dialogue—me to me, or rather my unconscious to my conscious mind—about what had and hadn't happened in the dream. This dialogue has been so helpful. For the first time I'm spending time and energy on myself in a special way. I give myself time to think, reflect, feel. It is almost as if I have given birth to a part of myself, a nurturing, questioning self that is able to go deeper into what I need. I've realized that this is an inner guide, what you call my resilience."

Chris's dream allowed her to begin exploring parts of herself that she had not consciously focused on before. In heeding the inner tension generated by her dream, Chris recognized a viewpoint, other than her waking knowledge, that was still very much her own. As she questioned the meaning of the dream, she made some discoveries that surprised her.

In our ensuing sessions together, Chris began to understand the coping strategies she had adopted as a child. Her mother was an invalid whose needs dominated the household. Chris was not really allowed to be a child, as the neediness of her mother forced her to become self-sufficient at an early age. Hence in the dream she sees her baby, her own childhood, taken from her by her mother, the gypsy, whom Chris experienced in the dream as she had as a child—not as a frail person, but as an all-powerful force.

What began as a troubling dream became, in fact, a new avenue of inquiry that unlocked many previously closed doors. Chris began to examine the new childhood memories kindled by her dream. As she spent more time with the images, feelings, and thoughts that her resilience evoked in her, Chris found that it grew stronger and more accessible. She began to work with it in other ways as well, to explore feelings and decisions in her life.

Visualizing Our Resilient Voice

For some women, their resilient voice appears as an image or a fantasy of what they would like to do or how they would like to handle a particular situation. They may actually envision themselves responding in a certain way, and this visual fantasy can be their guide in how to respond.

Judith had often found herself blocked when making decisions about what she needed and wanted. She said, "Usually I'd say, 'Oh, I don't care,' when in reality I just couldn't figure out what I wanted to do." She found that when she needed to make a decision, whether it was what to order for dinner or whether to continue swimming laps in the pool, the easiest way for her to decide was to stop, picture the choice in her mind, and see which way her visual fantasy took it.

"I've been surprised what happens when I see myself in a situation I am trying to make a decision about," said Judith. "One time when a friend asked me if I wanted to join her for lunch, I paused for a moment and saw myself running out of a restaurant. I said no to that invitation. Another time my son asked me if I would read him a story. I felt tired and inclined to say no, but when I pictured myself in the moment, I saw myself relaxed and cuddling my little boy. And so I said yes."

Over time, Judith has become more skilled at tuning into this part of who she is. Judith said, "It's like there is a private me that I rather enjoy. And the pleasure or confidence that I feel when I imagine enjoying myself or solving a problem gives me the permission to ask for what I want."

This sense of permission to ask for and arrange for what we need and want is the hallmark of our resilient voice. For in learning to listen to ourselves, in learning to hear our own answers about our needs and wants, we strengthen our understanding of the part of us that knows what we need to take care of ourselves. We are no longer kept apart from what nourishes us. The more we use this part of who we are, the easier and quicker it becomes to access it.

Using Your Resilient Voice

Listen to the voice or image in your mind the next time you need to make a decision—whether you want another cookie, need to work late, or want to set a limit with your child.

Pause for a moment. Ask yourself how to proceed and listen to the answers that come. Weigh which one feels right. Perhaps you'll hear an internal verbal response or feel a drop in tension as you consider a new option. Or perhaps you'll see yourself doing what you would really like to do.

Practice calling upon this part of you, your resilient voice, on a regular basis. Find out which of these three different avenues you use to perceive it: (1) Are you primarily auditory, so that you hear the right answer? (2) Are you primarily visual, so that you see yourself? (3) Are you primarily kinesthetic, so that you feel the right answers? For many people, resilience speaks through their unconscious. Do your dreams or daydreams provide clues? Keep this in mind as you work with the exercises in this book. Feel free to tailor the instructions to whatever works best for you.

Continue to cultivate this part of you by using it frequently. Use it throughout your day. Ask yourself what you need, and see which answer is the right one.

Other Voices

Childhood is a time of taking in, of observing and imitating, of listening to our parents, our teachers, our peers. From all these sources we internalize various beliefs and attitudes. These, too, often take the form of internal voices.

"Why is it so tough for me to make a decision?" Gwen asked me. "Every time I take a step forward I feel that I sabotage myself. I am so full of conflicting feelings and desires."

Gwen was an intelligent woman who had recently completed her sophomore year at college, but had difficulty deciding how to apply her education in a fulfilling career. Overprotected as a child, she had been trained to look to stronger adults for the answers, not to look inward for her own counsel.

I encouraged her to listen to the opinions that were warring inside of her and to write them out. In our next session she told me excitedly, "I took your advice and started writing out the dialogue just as I heard it inside my head. As I did, I realized that I could make out at least three distinct voices. Two of them I recognized as my older sister's and my father's voices; they were the ones telling me I couldn't succeed. My father's voice was telling me not to take chances, to go back to my old job at the supermarket, not to put myself in danger of failing. My sister's would chime in, saying who did I think I was anyway trying to do something better?

"But then I was aware of another voice debating with these stronger critical voices. I sensed that this softer, more compassionate voice was my own, expressing my side of the story—my opinions, my values, my dreams, my plans. There it is, I thought to myself. That's my resilient voice!"

Identifying the Dialogues

Pleased with this first discovery, Gwen continued to use this technique of writing out the dialogues and gradually found that she moved through the criticism and fears that kept her from making a decision. Gwen said, "Although it seemed gentler at first, my resilient voice was more sure, more convincing than the other voices, which were really only reflecting my fears and doubts." Gwen followed the counsel of her resilient voice to major in education and obtain her teaching certificate. The last time I saw her, she had just accepted a position teaching second grade.

As Gwen discovered, learning to listen to our resilient voice is not always an easy task. For as we try to isolate this one voice, we begin to hear the many other voices we have heard over the years—the voices of our parents, family members or close friends, perhaps social or religious authorities. In thinking through a course of action or response to a given situation, we may first encounter these other viewpoints. Until we learn to recognize them for what they are, they vie with our own voice, and we may give in to doing what others expect of us, rather than acting according to our own needs.

The process of understanding our resilient voice involves our ability to identify these other voices that inhabit the maze of our sometimes conflicting opinions and attitudes. In this way we can more effectively override their less helpful aspects and begin to focus more clearly on who we are and what is best in our lives for our fulfillment and happiness.

Distinguishing the Dialogue Within

At the top of a sheet of paper, write out a question you have about an event or incident that puzzles you or a course of action you have been unable to decide upon. For example:

- What do I want to do this summer?
- Why does seeing my mother always make me so mad?
- Why can't I make a commitment to my boyfriend?
- What is it that is keeping me from getting started on an exercise program?

Then write out each response that comes to mind, without censoring your ideas, without stopping to think. Continue to write for ten to fifteen minutes without a break.

Practice this exercise on a daily basis, if possible. After you have done this several times, read over all your answers. Do you recognize your resilient voice? Do you recognize the source of the other voices you recorded? Most people are amazed to see how internal voices represent actual people, such as a parent, sibling, or other important person in their life.

The more often you practice this exercise, the more readily you will be able to access your resilient voice.

Why We May Not Want to Listen

Listening inward will cause us also to confront our less familiar aspects, those qualities or memories we prefer to keep hidden from the world, perhaps even from ourselves. This is our dark side that houses what we find too painful, unsafe, or unacceptable to acknowledge. This may be our anger, rage, or neediness that we fear will alienate others. It may be parts of our personality we dislike, such as jealousy or inflexibility, or a role we played at a particular time in our lives. For many, it is the part of us that does not conform to the expectations of those we love.

Our dark side has to do with feelings and beliefs about ourselves. We realize early on that we do not always behave as we should. We are not always even-tempered, loving, and strong; at times we are angry, anxious, and vulnerable. Here we need to forgive ourselves for being so very human and come to understand and embrace those vulnerabilities. We all have limits to what we can do. Although this realization comes with age, I believe it is important for young women to learn that it is not shameful to have limits. It is an essential lesson we learn through our resilience.

While we instinctively distrust our dark side, this very part of us often contains our most powerful elements, those that are most uniquely our own. In suppressing these parts, we not only keep ourselves from using this personal power, but also expend psychic and emotional energy in doing so—energy which can be used more productively in our daily lives to accomplish the tasks before us.

If we are to be free to draw on our resilience, we need to develop the ability to speak about our dark side, to acknowledge and integrate these elements into our more pleasing qualities. In doing so, painful feelings can be reframed and resolved. We can begin to see unacceptable parts not as wrong or shameful, but as pieces of the puzzle of who we are. We can use the insight and skills we gain from our experiences, good and bad, to better understand what we need to do for ourselves in the future.

As we transform these negative aspects, they lose their hold over us; we are no longer held back by the pain or the discomfort of being who we are or being less than we would like. We gain a new power, a new control over our lives. We claim the power hidden in the dark side.

Through the Looking Glass: Reframing Our Negative Experiences

Many women suffer shame or unresolved pain because of events in the past. We are reluctant to reexamine the memories of difficult or traumatic experiences because we will also recall the negative feelings and messages associated with them. When we stress our resilience in surviving them, however, we can change these feelings and messages. This new perspective can help us to look at our experiences from the inside out, as sources of strength and insight rather than vulnerability and shame. We have new options to explore.

Rachel was a young woman who came to see me for depression. One session, she told me of the Thanksgiving when she was eleven. Her alcoholic mother had invited relatives over but was unable to prepare the holiday meal. Rather than have her mother face the recriminations of their visiting relatives, Rachel took it upon herself to prepare a complete Thanksgiving dinner for her family. I was struck by the resourcefulness and courage of this feat.

The pain of this memory was evident as Rachel recounted it. Yet rather than asking her about this aspect of the event, I asked, "How did you know how to cook a turkey and make stuffing at eleven years old?" Rachel looked at me blankly.

I went on, "That took quite a bit of planning, skill, and perseverance. How did you know how to do it?"

She faintly smiled and said, "I guess I was pretty smart."

It was clear she had never considered this incident in such a way. In her memory, the shame and fear that had motivated her at the time remained uppermost in her mind. The positive and worthy aspects of the event had been lost beneath these negative emotions.

As we talked about this incident, she realized that even at that early age she had possessed the wisdom to keep her family together and create a Thanksgiving dinner that corresponded to her image of what it should be. She had recognized her needs and learned the skills necessary to take care of herself and her family.

This opened up a new avenue of exploration for Rachel. Without denying the hardship of her early experiences, she began to see the choices she had made that had brought her safely through those painful years.

"I began to see myself no longer as the victim of my childhood, but as a survivor." said Rachel. "For the first time I recognized the strengths and abilities I have developed along the way."

Viewed from that perspective, this experience and others began to take on a new meaning for her. She saw the other choices she had made which had consistently brought her closer to what she needed and began to see the pattern of control that she had unconsciously exerted on her life. Her sense of powerlessness, a major factor in her depression, no longer seemed overwhelming.

If we have come to see ourselves as victims, damaged by the circumstances of our lives, recognizing our resilience can help us to see instead that we are survivors. Like Rachel, we can use our resilience to review the past and see, perhaps for the first time, the unique blend of opportunity and challenge we experienced and the value we have made from it.

While all experience teaches us, our childhood experiences remain the most influential in the formation of our identity and resilience. We will look further at the role these early lessons play in chapter 4.

Redefining the Dark Side
The dark side for many women is their rebellious side. This part of us houses our nonconforming aspects that challenge what we experience around us. It is fashioned from our reaction to the expectations we perceive from our family and the greater society. This sense of difference may fuel our beliefs about our unworthiness or lack of desirability and lead to feelings of self-hate and rejection.

These feelings, too, can be reframed when we come to look at them through the perspective of our resilience. Once we look past our discomfort and other people's judgment of us, we can gain the courage to explore other choices and beliefs about ourselves. Once free of others' narrow definitions of what is right and wrong, we can come to a new appreciation of our own personality.

When Cynthia married Tom, she felt pulled in two directions. She hadn't realized until then how different the life Tom wanted was from that of her family.

Her family had lived in New York since the 1850s, building careers in public service: the ministry, education, social work, and municipal government. They were generous, hardworking, career-oriented people. Cynthia was proud of her family's contributions and planned to follow in their path. Like her grandmother, she had earned a degree in early childhood education.

Tom was a writer. Midway to his master's in English literature, he decided it was more important to concentrate on his novel. He quit school and worked part time while Cynthia finished her degree.

After graduation, they moved to central Washington where the cost of living was far lower than on the East Coast. Tom found a job as a reporter for the local newspaper, and Cynthia took a job at an elementary school.

Cynthia said, "My parents tolerated our move to Washington as part of our need to find ourselves, as my mother said. Once the baby was born, however, the questions began: When are you going to grow up, take a real job, take your place in society? They dropped broad hints that they expected a visit soon. Were we planning to move? Didn't we want to be closer to our families who could help with the baby?

"I began to see myself in a different way, too," Cynthia said. "Before, I loved the life we'd made in Washington. The town itself was quiet and clean. The sense of community was strong, and I felt blessed to be part of it. We didn't have much in the way of possessions, and we didn't really miss them on a day-to-day basis.

"But suddenly I found myself thinking, What are you doing with your life? My sister had her doctorate and was already publishing articles in academic journals. My brother, a district attorney, boasted a very good salary and terrific benefits. Tom and I had none of this.

"It wasn't anything I could put my finger on, but I began to feel that everything around us was small, unimportant. I regretted being so far from home. The fact is, I had never given much thought to doing things any differently from my family until then." Cynthia found it hard to quiet the voices inside about her selfishness and irresponsibility because she had made different choices than her brother and sister.

"Actually, I wasn't even aware of this running dialogue in my mind until one day while on summer break I sat on the front step in the sun with my daughter. I told her, 'Aren't we lucky? My mom and I couldn't do this when I was a girl.' Suddenly everything fell into place: I was living in a way that I had never been able to as a child. No wonder it felt so strange at times. My mother wasn't home with me; she had a career that involved travel and long office hours. While we were close and I was always provided for, my mother and I never had time to sit out on a summer afternoon. In New York, my family didn't know the neighbors very well or have time to participate in community events the way Tom and I do. Here, there was none of the pollution or crime and violence my sister contends with in Boston.

"I realized Tom and I have made a life that isn't based on money, public works, or prestige, but on different values. It's a simpler, quieter life. Sure, it was hard to give up my old dreams of living in New York in my grandfather's house. But I see now that's all they were: dreams. It wasn't what I wanted for my life."

In recognizing our uniqueness we can step outside the definitions others have given to us. We begin to see our fundamental expressions of personality and choice in new ways. Cynthia's choice of lifestyle became a source of personal pride and happiness. Once removed from the context of "right" and "wrong" behavior, we see that what we thought of as wrong is actually only different. Recognizing that difference can be a turning point in the validation of our own individuality.

The Anger in Our Dark Side

Most women experience difficulty feeling and expressing anger. Our society teaches us that women should be pliant, accepting, nurturing, and positive. Feelings of anger are not appropriate. Many women feel this pressure and work to fulfill the expectation at the expense of their true feelings. They begin to deny not only their needs, but also the very expressions of hurt and anger when their needs are not met.

At times these feelings make women feel unworthy or ashamed because their emotions are not congruent with their identity or experiences. They begin to assume blame for being different. This tension between inner reality and outer expectation frequently results in displaced anger that protects others but depresses a woman's ability to access her resilience.

Despite the stereotypes, anger is part of life and part of human experience. When we recognize and channel it, anger can give us the power to change a situation, meet challenges, or try new possibilities. Whether this anger inspires us to leave a dead-end job, break off a bad relationship, or recognize that we are too stressed, it tells us change is needed. We gain power from our emerging understanding that there are alternatives to the present situation that we can pursue.

In the mid-1960s, Linda wanted to major in geology, a most unusual choice for a young woman, she was told. But Linda could see many old ways crumbling and the beginning of a new era. She demonstrated against the Vietnam War, stopped wearing a bra, and rebelled in many other personal ways.

Linda said, "I was furious with the discrimination against women I encountered in trying to get into a so-called man's field. I was enraged by patronizing professors who would call me Miss and refuse to take me seriously. The more I tried to play by their rules and still get an education, the harder it became for me to contain my anger.

"I finally was forced to recognize the futility of it when a professor scoffed at my question during a class discussion and refused to answer it. I was so angry I stood up right then and there and told him what I thought of him. I reminded him none too nicely that my tuition paid his salary. Once he recovered from his shock, he ordered me to leave the class and gave me a two-week suspension. Despite my excellent course work, I received a barely passing grade."

Some of Linda's friends told her to organize a boycott of the professor's classes. Linda thought about how much fun it would be to ridicule him the way he had her. She said, "Then I thought, What would it get me? Why waste all that energy when it won't get me any closer to my career goals?

"I realized that if I tried to stay with geology, I would spend all my energy just fighting to be heard. It wasn't a battle I was interested in, and perhaps wasn't one I could win." This realization led Linda to pursue a new path.

Linda reevaluated her goals and switched her major to political science. She realized her personal interest in change and revolution were right in line with the subject. She went on to become an environmental activist, a profession that would use both her interest in the natural sciences and her natural temper as a fighter.

"Today I spend my anger in more constructive ways," said Linda. "Rather than fighting small, futile battles, I use my energy to accomplish something. I use it to speak out and rally others to important issues.

"I realize now that I have befriended the anger that used to get me into so much trouble. It's as if the more I tried to conceal it, the more unpredictable and uncontrollable it became. I know how to use it to accomplish what's important to me. It no longer rules me."

Like all emotions, anger is a clue to what is going on inside. As we recognize our anger and the situations in which it arises, we can learn about ourselves. Resilience gives us the courage to acknowledge and claim our anger and turn it to our advantage.

Transforming Our Dark Side

Recognizing and working with our dark side can be a valuable tool in the development of our resilience, for it is often in our dark side that the stresses which contribute to our resilience can be seen most clearly. We can see what forces have helped to shape our resilience and more consciously use these forces to help us address other issues in this part of ourselves.

Rebecca was terribly jealous of her husband Ted's attention to other women at any time, but it was particularly appalling for her when they went to parties. Here she would be racked by feelings of betrayal, self-pity, rage, and humiliation. When they went home after the party, she would hurl accusations at him, leading to horrendous fights. Afterward she would be repentant and beg his forgiveness, but her rages over time took their toll on the marriage.

"I just couldn't seem to make myself stop. It was like I was possessed and out to destroy Ted and our relationship," said Rebecca. Eventually it felt easier not to be together and they separated.

After their split, Rebecca's jealousy began to diminish. It felt less dangerous to consider the feelings that led to their separation. Gradually Rebecca understood that her jealousy of Ted was more about her feeling anxious in public situations than about Ted's behavior. She realized that when she went to a party, she needed a special type of attention and reassurance from her partner to help her overcome her fear. Much of her anger at Ted came from her feeling that she could not ask him for the support she needed.

In trying to be independent and live up to her own expectations, she held fast to the notion that self-reliance meant that she should not ask for what she needed. Rather than admit her own vulnerability, she preferred to accuse Ted of wrongdoing. Yet it was her own unacknowledged sense of helplessness that caused her rages.

Rebecca then began to look for this neediness in other situations. "I saw patterns of behavior I'd never noticed," she said. "In fact, there were many occasions when I felt anxious, and each time I covered this anxiety with other emotions that I could externalize. Once I was aware of this pattern, my anxiety became less unpredictable and more easy to control.

"It was as if knowing what it was and when it occurred took away the sense that it was larger than life. I realized that my rages had more to do with me and my ability to handle my anxiety than with Ted's behavior. I could make different choices as to how to deal with my feelings." The couple entered marital counseling and were able to reconcile.

It is in the process of identifying these darker, less acceptable aspects of self and in making peace with them that we find our own voice. In this way our dark side is a valuable ally. It can tell us what is ours and ours alone—a vision, a point of view derived from our own way. It is not apart from our life, a separate being, but integral to it.

Until we learn the lessons of our dark side, we live with less than we are and could be.

Dark Side

The next time you are angry, confused, or just feeling racked by emotion in general, take a few moments to define these feelings. If possible, record your answers in writing. Ask your resilient voice

- How am I feeling?
- Why am I feeling like this?
- What can I do to resolve this?
- What do my feelings tell me about what I need?

Once you have calmed down, look over your responses. Ask your resilient self to add any new information that may have occurred to you. See how you can use this information for needed change. Does it prompt you to action, like Anne's leaving a family reunion? Or provide a change in perspective, such as Rebecca's realization that a major part of her jealousy came from her own fears?

Remember, the dark side has valuable information for us. See what your dark side is telling you.

CHAPTER 3

Patterns of Resilience

Each of us has developed natural resilience to a greater or lesser degree. In first becoming conscious of your own resilient qualities, it is important to recognize the extent to which you already draw on these strengths and the areas in which you do so. How you presently use your resilience depends on the challenges and reinforcement you experienced in childhood, adolescence, and early adulthood, and how you have come to understand these experiences.

In talking about these differences and their implications for personal development, I have found it useful to think in terms of six different styles of resilience. It is important to keep in mind that the categories that follow are not value judgments, nor do they indicate a woman's potential or need for change. They are only a general characterization of the ways in which a woman tends to use her resilience.

1. *Women of balanced resilience* are capable in many areas; their flexibility allows them to enjoy an easy give and take. Women of balanced resilience can use their resilience to become more conscious of their strengths and to tackle challenges.

2. *Women of undeveloped resilience* are tentative, inexperienced. They leave decision making to others. Alone, they are apt to feel incomplete. These women can use resilience to learn to make

their own decisions and come to terms with themselves and to take responsibility.

3. *Women of paradoxical resilience* feel as if they are two people. They are liable to be anxious in situations where they feel unskilled, shamed, or inadequate, but they are quite competent in their areas of known expertise. These women can use resilience to realize that their skills in one area can apply in other areas and to learn new skills.

4. *Women of self-contained resilience* are isolated. Their identity is defined by being extremely competent, so they constantly feel they must do it all, with little or no help from others. These women can use resilience to develop flexibility and discover security in letting others in.

5. *Women of overwhelmed resilience* feel shame and self-contempt. They are unable to use resources on their own behalf. These women can use their resilience to recognize their well-developed survival skills and to use these skills to meet their own needs on a daily basis and develop self-esteem.

6. *Women of stellar resilience* tend to be defined by their knowledge of having survived trauma. They are vigilant about keeping on track no matter what the area: personal development, professional success, relationships, and so forth. These women can use resilience to integrate their past and present, and to learn to open up and let others take charge once in a while.

Balanced Resilience

Balanced resilience is usually found in women who have led reasonably happy lives, without major loss or trauma. Often raised in families that offered protection and guidance, women of balanced resilience have had less need to draw consciously on their inner resilience. Their challenges have been the normal transitions of growing up and learning to cope with life. They tend to bring their strengths to bear equally in all areas of their lives.

The task of a woman with balanced resilience is to learn more about her resilience and to use this part of herself to enhance her development. Life is full of challenges: from doing well in school, surviving adolescence, and separating from one's family, to finding a partner, building a family, establishing a career, and learning to deal with growing older. Facing these challenges with the assistance and guidance of our resilience allows us to accomplish these transitions less painfully and to perceive them as rewarding, even as adventures. These life crises can be used as opportunities to grow and flourish, and to discover deeper meaning in our lives.

Peggy has always defined herself as average. She said, "I grew up on a ranch with six sisters and brothers. We were all taught to love the land. Each of us had jobs to do for the family. Family life revolved around the needs of us kids, the cattle, and the ranch. By no means wealthy, we were comfortable. The feeling that there was enough for everyone was much more important than material wealth.

"Our mother typified this by saying, 'What kids need is love.' So even when we went through years of drought or when money was tight, we knew that our parents loved us and that we would get through these problems together. Our roots were firmly established in our family and in the earth we all loved."

When Peggy thinks of her childhood, she smiles. "It was great growing up in the West, in Missoula, Montana. I graduated from high school, went to junior college, and married at the standard age of twenty-one. I gave birth to my first child at twenty-three. I loved being a mother."

Life had presented few surprises for Peggy. "I raised the kids, and when I had to, I went to work part time," she said. "The boys got jobs to help pay for their school expenses. Then my husband Al was laid off, so I went to work full time in an insurance company. To my surprise, I was steadily advanced and am now an adjuster. Al was able to find another line of work. The boys married and settled near by. We were set.

"Until recently, that is. Al is being transferred out of state away from the boys and their families. Now I'm at a crisis point. I've managed other transitions in life, but this one doesn't seem fair. I love being a mother and grandmother. It was bad enough to go to work full time when the boys were still in school, but now we'll be fourteen hundred miles away. Yes, I know that we need to go, but it hurts. And to tell you the truth, at my age I'm afraid to move and start over in a new community. My grandson Jake tells me I'll just have to sprout wings so I can come back often. But I think he really has a point. I need a new way to take care of myself, a new way to see myself to accomplish this move."

Like most women of balanced resilience, Peggy's personal power has been largely unconscious. Not given to introspection, Peggy has taken for granted her ability to cope with life's demands. Peggy's resilience has been a natural outgrowth of her life, a comfortable part of who she was. Life has challenged her, but not beyond what she felt equipped to handle.

Now that she is confronting a major challenge, she needs to draw upon her flexibility, her personal power, to make this major transition. To accomplish this with the same equanimity that she has had other transition points, she needs to be more conscious of her own ability to withstand change and make the best of it. By discovering her resilience and using it to counsel and guide her through this difficult time, Peggy can change this challenge into a new possibility for internal growth and development.

Undeveloped Resilience

Undeveloped resilience is common in women who are passive, tentative, or inexperienced in owning their power to make choices. In this way women of undeveloped resilience resemble children who have not learned to anticipate their own needs or to make their own way.

These women have been so overprotected that they have little sense of the world or of themselves. They have been taught to depend on others to take care of them or make the important decisions for them. As a result, they never see themselves as complete. If a woman relies on a partner as her "better half," she may always feels anxious that her partner will leave. When her partner does leave, a woman with undeveloped resilience may feel that she has lost an essential part of her own identity.

Laura is a woman of undeveloped resilience. "I guess I've gone through my life without making a decision for myself," said Laura. "I never had to, until my divorce. Before that, I did everything by the rules. The sad thing is, the rules didn't protect me from this pain."

Laura grew up as the second of four girls in rural South Carolina in a rigidly religious family. "My parents raised us with the knowledge that they and God had the answers to our problems," she said. "I grew up to depend on my parents to solve whatever trouble came my way. They were loving, kind, and gentle people. We had a simple life and never lacked anything. I went to a fundamentalist college that stepped in where my parents left off in taking care of me and my decisions."

In college Laura met a young man and they married. She said, "I always looked to him to provide the framework for my life. I always felt at a loss when he wasn't home. I did everything I could to please him. I cooked the foods he liked, dressed the way he preferred, didn't wear makeup or perfume. We never danced or listened to rock music because he was as religious as I was. I quit school when we married to let him be the provider. I let him make all the decisions.

"So three children later and pregnant with our fourth, I was stunned when he said he was leaving me for someone else. I couldn't even imagine how he had met someone else, but it turned out she was someone at work he'd been seeing for several years. All that overtime he was required to do turned out to be her.

"I was devastated. I felt my world was crumbling around me. Nothing in my life had prepared me for this. If I had been alone, I might have killed myself, but I couldn't do that to my children. I just had to find another way.

"With all the stress I was under, I had a miscarriage in my fourth month. This may have been God's way, but I blame it on my husband. Suddenly I realized that I had to get myself together in a way that I never had to before. I had to earn a living; I had to provide a family life for my children. I had to survive."

Laura is finding that she needs to develop her resilience. In her difficult situation, she is fortunate to have warm and loving support from others in her church, but she still has much to do alone. She is hurt and bewildered, but is using this part of herself to grow, to challenge old beliefs and to take the next step.

"It's pretty hard right now; the kids and I have to learn how to do everything differently. But hard as it is, there is some part of me that loves it, too. I feel good doing things for myself and my family. I like the feeling of accomplishment. For the first time in my life, I'm beginning to know what self-sufficiency means."

The task facing a woman with such undeveloped resilience is to begin to experiment with being independent. To do this, she must find safe situations with ample support for taking risks. Small initial steps are in order, such as dressing to please herself and changing the way she organizes her time. In seeing what happens as she makes choices, she can begin to nurture her own inner resilience.

Paradoxical Resilience

Paradoxical resilience describes women who use their resilience in particular areas of their lives but not in others. Many women are successful at work where they hold positions of responsibility and are skilled at making choices. They feel pride, even a sense of accomplishment, in this role for them.

Yet these same women are utterly different in their personal lives. Although they are decisive at work, they are unable to make decisions at home. While they are assertive on the job, they may even allow themselves to be subjected to abuse at home. They are unable to apply the skills that gain them promotions at work to their personal relationships, needs, or preferences.

Other women with paradoxical resilience manage a home, juggle the needs of children and spouse, participate in community events, and serve in positions of responsibility in volunteer organizations. Yet these women feel that they cannot compete in the professional world. They see their skills as an expression of the love they have for their family, rather than a reflection of their personal resources.

Both groups of women need to explore their individual strengths and skills and see how these can be applied in other areas of their lives. In doing so, they can own their personal strengths and talents and begin to define themselves on the basis of who they are inside, not just by their capacity to perform specific roles in particular settings.

Sue feels that she lives two lives. Professionally, she is a resourceful and competent accounts executive with an advertising firm. At twenty-eight, she has already risen within the company and is told she is being groomed for bigger and better opportunities. Sue is known for her energy, her ability to win new accounts, and her attention to detail. She looks and acts the part of a young, successful career woman.

At home she lives with Ron, a twenty-two-year-old student. In her honest moments, Sue knows Ron will never finish college. But she spends her time trying to make him happy—a useless effort, she knows, although she doesn't dare to let her frustration show for she is desperately afraid that he will leave her. Being alone is the worst fate imaginable for her.

To see her at home is not to see the vital young woman she is at work. At home, she is anxious, unsure of herself. She is afraid that if she is assertive, Ron will feel threatened and leave her.

Sue said, "My parents are upset at my living with Ron and constantly criticize him, which only forces me to defend him. They wanted something better for me, they say. They are caring people who always encouraged me, while simultaneously undermining their praise. For example, I'd study long hours to get A's. My parents were proud of my A's but criticized me for working too hard for them. They always told me I was beautiful, but no boyfriend was quite right for me. They thought I made poor choices."

Sue's childhood was a series of contradictions, so it is no wonder that she reflects this by the unevenness of her growth. At work she feels she can ask for what she needs and wants, even demand it. She advocates for herself. But at home these same tasks and skills seem alien to her.

The task of paradoxically resilient women is to explore ways to apply their strengths more evenly in their lives. Owning their resilience will cause them to confront the self-defeating beliefs they learned in childhood about women's competence and capabilities. As they free themselves of these ideas, they can begin to develop a new self-image based on realistic information about who they really are.

Self-Contained Resilience

Women of self-contained resilience compromise their resilience with inflexibility. They have had to be so resilient for so long, the positive aspects of resilience have been exaggerated. They learned early in life to distrust others and so believe they can only rely on themselves. As a result, they become isolated, unable to branch out. They spend their time and energy shoring up their defenses, ready for the next attack. They are so fearful of being vulnerable, they can never let down their guard.

A woman of self-contained resilience can be very successful by external standards. She can look great, meet deadlines, negotiate, and get the job done. She develops certain skills to perfection but tends to neglect her needs in other areas in her life. On the inside, she may be barren of feeling, a stranger even to herself. She may enter relationships only to find her partners leave her, saying that she was too closed off or that she would not let them love her.

Carla is a bright, attractive banker. At forty-two she became a vice president in a major bank specializing in international finance. She works hard and puts in long hours, both of which have paid off with career success.

On the surface she is friendly and exudes competence. In fact, her competence defines Carla. She works at this part of herself morning, noon, and night. It is the only part she knows. She socializes for work, but not on a personal level. "I feel that I either lost the art of friendship or perhaps never developed it," said Carla. "I know that I frequently disappoint my family by being so unavailable. I am always late, only spending a little time with them, or I decline invitations outright."

Carla's childhood appeared stable. Her mother was a teacher and her father a moderately successful business man. They lived in a suburb of Memphis in a home that they still own.

But the outward stability was deceptive. Carla explained, "My mother was what psychologists call narcissistic; everything has to be for and about her. I became aware of this for the first time when I noticed my mother playing with her grandchildren. She kept dancing around saying, 'Look at me! Look at me!' Her only way of engaging them was by their paying attention to her.

"My father was known as the problem in the family. His moods would alternate between depression and rage, the latter directed verbally at my mother, whom he constantly tried to please and never could.

"My younger sister, Nina, was the preferred daughter. As the older sibling I was always encouraged to give in to her because I was supposed to be too mature to act out my feelings."

Carla soon learned that her feelings did not account for much in her family, but her ability to handle difficult situations did. This is what she has carried with her into adult life.

Carla has not had the opportunity to branch out and develop other parts of herself. When asked about her personal goals, she is quick to quip, "Men? I can understand why a man needs a woman, I just can't understand why a woman needs a man. My biological clock? It stopped working a long time ago."

Carla was able to keep her life in perfect order until she was recently diagnosed with cancer. At this point she has just begun to confront the feelings that she had previously ignored. She is beginning to see that she will need to give up her inflexibility to weather this new reality in her life. She wants to explore more of her personal side and has already begun to use her resilience to grow and nurture other parts of her being.

The tasks that lie before women of self-contained resilience involve using their well-developed resilience to explore other parts of themselves. Just as their insight and well-honed skills have been developed to bolster an air of competence in their lives, they need to learn relax and trust that others will meet their needs. In doing this, their isolation will subside, leading to a richer and ultimately more rewarding life.

Overwhelmed Resilience

Women of overwhelmed resilience have been overly challenged and survived their traumatic childhood by accepting the blows and threats of others, rather than finding a way to fend them off. These women have survived, but only by paying a great price for their survival: the sacrifice of their self-esteem and positive self-image.

Rather than learning to see adversity as a challenge or an adventure, they have learned to view themselves as the cause of the difficulties they encounter. They think of themselves with shame. While the primary direction of resilience is survival, enabling us to discover and draw upon inner strengths, to retain optimism, and to reach out for help and support, shame can make us wish that we were never born or that we could simply disappear. The overwhelmed person may feel helpless and withdraw from situations; hopelessness may pervade her life. Where resilience finds safe ways to express feelings, shame often results in unexpressed feelings. Where strong resilience provides an identity that says, "I can face this problem," shame states, "I am the problem."

The task before these women is to learn of their strengths, wisdom, and worthiness. It is often a long and arduous process, going back to the origins of their pain and making conscious the conclusions they reached in childhood about themselves and the world. As adults, the painful conclusions that helped to make their survival possible can now be challenged and discarded in favor of new, more appropriate, and nurturing beliefs.

Donna is a woman of overwhelmed resilience. At thirty-seven, she is an attractive, outgoing, and hard-working graphic artist. Devoting a great deal of her energy to her work, she prides herself on the value she devotes to friendship. "When one of my friends needs me, I am there," says Donna. Between her two passions—work and friendship— she has very little time to develop romantic interests. Virtually all her friends are gay men, so she always enjoys male company, but at the same time she is lonely.

Beneath her vivacious facade is her shame. One area of shame concerns her own needs. It is all right to be the one who gives, but

Donna feels it is wrong for her to be needy. She is also ashamed of her need for a sexual relationship with a man.

The reason for this is buried in her past. When Donna was a child, her mother was depressed. When Donna was fourteen, her mother attempted suicide and was hospitalized for several weeks. Donna's father, who had always been flirtatious with his daughter, began to make sexual advances, usually as she comforted him when he returned home after seeing her mother in the hospital. Donna initially excused his behavior as justifiable "upset," but after a while she began to blame herself. Unconsciously, this was safer than feeling rage at her mother for abandoning her through illness or at her father for abandoning his role as her parent to become her lover.

Unable to reconcile her awakening sexual feelings and her own neediness with the situation she confronted, Donna experienced increasing self-contempt. She hated her sexual feelings because they were dangerous; sexuality made people change and "turn on you." And she hated her neediness. It overwhelmed others and drove the people she most needed, her parents, away. After her mother returned home, Donna was torn between caring for her mother and comforting her father while dissuading his sexual overtures. She resolved this difficult balance psychologically by avoiding women's friendships and having only male friends who had no sexual interest in her.

As a woman whose resilience has been overwhelmed, Donna walks through life feeling that her own needs are wrong. Rather than resilience, she feels shame and self-hatred. She has come to feel unworthy of the nurturing and love she so readily gives to others. She does not believe she deserves to ask others for comfort nor to have her own needs met. These are the beliefs she needs to challenge as an adult.

Healing an overwhelmed personality involves changing the way a person thinks about the world. This is a long and difficult process, but the potential gain far outweighs the pain. With time and support, a woman with overwhemed resilience can develop stellar resilience.

Stellar Resilience

This resilience pattern is produced as a means of survival against great challenges. It is developed in individuals who have had to withstand extraordinary circumstances. Women of stellar resilience are those whose competence, security, and self-fulfillment belie the chaos, tragedy, or hardship they have experienced in their early lives. As adults, they may have achieved a happy home life despite an unhappy childhood. They may have money and security despite impoverished beginnings. They may seem happy and at peace with the world, despite having suffered terrible tragedy.

Despite their obvious success, however, many women of stellar resilience are haunted by the feeling that even now they are not "normal" or capable of living a normal life, because their lives have been abnormal, even extraordinary. They are plagued with the idea that they have no way to create a normal life for themselves or their family because they have never experienced a typical home or upbringing. As a result, they may feel damaged, scarred, different, even tainted.

Many women of stellar resilience feel they have paid a high price for their survival. When they look at themselves in the context of their family of origin, for example, they often feel separated, uncomfortable, and perhaps angry. They may experience "survivor's guilt" for having survived and thrived when others they love have not. They often feel they exist in limbo between their present accomplishments, which they can't quite own, and the past, which they have overcome.

Their sense of self contains not only the positive values of their childhood but also their knowledge of their ability to withstand and master pain. This awareness may compromise their vision of the future; they need to learn to move beyond the anticipation and mastery of pain, and learn to use their energies to develop a more enjoyable present. Instead of constantly worrying about surviving the next disaster, they need to learn to anticipate pleasurable outcomes.

Maria is a woman of stellar resilience. She is a social worker and is recognized as a leading authority on child abuse. She is married, the mother of two boys and a girl, and considers herself successful in her life. When viewed from the outside her life is ideal: a two-career family, a nice home in the suburbs of Chicago, and healthy children who do well in school. But Maria is plagued by the idea that all she has created is a sham.

Maria came from an Italian and Polish family of five children. Her father worked hard to provide a good home, but he was killed in a car accident that also killed Maria's oldest brother. Her mother had a terrible time coping with her losses, and the children were sent to live with relatives for a time. Maria went to live with an aunt who owned a small drug store.

Maria was required to come home after school every day to work behind the counter and sweep up after hours. Despite her grief, Maria discovered she enjoyed dealing with customers and that they in turn liked her. She began to realize how well she got along with others, including teachers and, later, employers and clients.

Maria and her siblings returned to live with their mother shortly before her remarriage. Maria said, "My stepfather disliked us children, and our home became unbearable. Life was a nightmare of disorder and cruelty. My brother became an addict. Eventually he was thrown out of the house to live on the streets. My sisters did somewhat better. They have remained in Chicago, in the old neighborhood. Both married blue-collar workers, are raising large families, and, like our mother, struggle to make ends meet.

"My sisters see their lives as defined by their childhood. Not me. My early responsibilities at the drug store taught me that I had other options in life. In high school I found a job and worked hard to prove myself.

"Somehow, though, it's too easy to say that hard work and education alone allowed me to escape," sighed Maria, the recipient of many scholarships. "I think there was some strength in my chaotic family that allowed me to survive the poverty and abuse and be able to use it in my life. Some of my strength came from my experience living with my aunt after my father's death. I saw I could work hard and achieve something. When I did, people perceived me in a new way. I could be more than that poor kid without a dad."

Maria also benefited from her relationship with her youngest sister. "After our mother remarried, life was hell. We both vowed to leave as soon as possible and create a better life for ourselves and our children. Together we daydreamed and blue-skied about what our life would be like. I think that the support we gave each other allowed us both to see beyond our childhood reality, and having seen what we wanted, we were both freed to go after it. The only difference between our dreams was that my sister was going to marry someone to take care or her. I was going to do it on my own."

Both women's dreams have come true. "My sister is taken care of," said Maria. "She hasn't left the old neighborhood, but she seems to be doing just fine. I have left and feel like an alien when I return. Now that I am out, I do not know where I belong. People look at me as if I'm a freak.

"I feel accomplished but not connected. I have been able to deal with the past abuse by my stepfather, but it has been difficult to find a new relationship with him. Yes, I can lecture, I can write, but I still struggle with my feelings—about my father and my brothers, how our family was torn apart, and my sense that there is nowhere that I belong."

Many women of stellar resilience feel a need to give back to those who gave to them and often enter the helping fields: nursing, teaching, social work, and psychology. Or they may turn their considerable energy to humanitarian causes, such as world peace, environmental preservation, or the protection of children. As a result, they are vulnerable to giving too much of themselves, sacrificing their energy and identity in helping others. They need to retain enough of their resources for themselves and enjoy the rare luxury of nurturing themselves as they nurture others. This can be their gift to themselves, the ability to enjoy what they often unselfishly give to others—a sense that life can be different and hold positive rewards.

Your Own Resilience Profile

These six basic patterns of resilience are designed as general descriptions only. In reality, our personal style of resilience and the areas in which we experience satisfaction or problems are more complex than the categories represented here. Most individuals find that they have characteristics of two or more areas, but that one comes closest to describing the way they use their resilience in their life. These categories prove to be a useful way to define areas of strength, areas of difficulty, and areas for growth.

Your *resilience profile* allows you to see the ways in which your resilience presently functions in your life. What are your strengths? What areas can be improved? How can you apply your personal power to new areas of your life? This simple assessment will highlight the areas in which you have already completed the most amount of work and allow you to see areas on which you may want to concentrate. Its purpose is not to tell you what to do, but to point out some options for either furthering the development of your resilience or using it more consciously.

The short assessments on the next pages are designed to help you determine your style of resiliency. Answer the ten italicized questions under each type of resiliency with a yes or no. Each question is further explained with examples.

Balanced Resilience

To determine your degree of balanced resilience ask yourself:

1. *Do you know your major strengths?* For example, are you knowledgeable about what you can and cannot do? Do you develop your strengths both at work and at home?

2. *Do you tend to focus on your strengths?* For example, do you like the parts of you that are strong? Are you proud of these aspects? Do you take time for them? Do you make time for hobbies—i.e., if you are athletic, do you make time for sports? or if you are a good gardener, do you garden?

3. *Do you feel you can set limits on others which allow your needs to be satisfied?* For example, is it okay to come first? Can you delay your child's, spouse's, or co-workers' requests so that you can complete what you are doing?

4. *Do you feel your childhood adequately prepared you for your adult life?* For example, do the expectations that you developed as a child match what you have come to know as an adult? Do you feel that you were given good role

47

models for adulthood? Do you feel sustained and even nurtured in your adulthood by the memories of the past?

5. *Did you feel protected as a child within your family?* For example, were your needs acknowledged and met? Were your feelings and thoughts listened to and respected? Did you feel loved and cared for?

6. *Do you use the information your family taught you in your daily life?* For example, do you draw upon the lessons you learned as a child? Do you feel a connection between the past and the present?

7. *Do you feel you had an average childhood?* For example, do you feel that your childhood was fairly uneventful? Looking back upon your childhood, are you unable to find any major problems that caused you undue stress?

8. *Do you like yourself?* For example, when you think of yourself, do you smile? Do you take care of yourself? Do you treat yourself the way you would treat a good friend?

9. *Do you feel that you are friendly to yourself?* For example, do you make demands upon yourself which are possible for you to meet? Do you treat yourself with respect, allowing yourself to say no to tasks that you are too tired to do or tasks that are unappealing?

10. *Do you use your resourcefulness and flexibility to accomplish your goals in life?* For example, do you allow yourself to be creative on your own behalf in meeting your needs? Do you reserve enough energy to allow yourself to be successful in achieving those objectives that are important to you, even if they are important only to you?

Total "Yes" answers (0-10) under Balanced Resilience _____

Undeveloped Resilience

To determine your degree of undeveloped resilience, ask yourself the following questions:

1. *Do you feel that you were overprotected as a child?* For example, did you feel smothered as a child? In looking back on your childhood, do you feel it was stifling or suffocating? Were you sheltered from taking responsibility for the consequences of your actions?

2. *Were you rarely given opportunities as a child to make decisions for yourself?* For example, were you given a set of rules to which you adhered, which kept you from learning how to think for yourself? Were you discouraged from learning how the world was, learning only to see it in a particular way?

3. *Was your dependence on others cultivated?* For example, were you constantly told that only your parents knew what was best for you? Were you made fearful of being on your own? Were you made to feel that you were incompetent to be on your own?

4. *Do you feel that your ability to plan and set goals for yourself is undeveloped?* For example, do you find it difficult to determine if an action is in your best interest? Is it hard for you to foresee consequences when they affect you? Are you shy about asking others to help you? Do you have problems rallying your resources?

5. *Do you depend now on someone else to make you whole?* For example, do you feel that your worth is tied to your caring for others? Do you fear that if a loved one leaves, you will be less than you are now? Do you think of your loved one as your "better half"?

6. *Do you find little opportunity in your life to experiment with independence?* For example, do you find yourself hiding behind the opinions of another, fearful of expressing your own? Do you devalue your own life experiences? Are you so afraid of being wrong or incompetent that you fear acting?

7. *Do you feel unequipped to take care of yourself?* For example, do you feel you know very little of what you need

or how to go about having these needs taken care of? Do you feel that others know more of what you need than you do? Do you expect others to know you so well that you do not need to speak up for yourself?

8. *Do you feel that others know more of the answers in life than you do?* For example, do you more readily turn to another for advice than seek your own counsel? Do you usually discount your opinion if someone else has a stronger opinion?

9. *Do you feel you function less as your own best friend than you would like to?* For example, are you more critical of yourself than you are of others? Are you frequently nicer to others than you are to yourself? Do you more readily make excuses for someone else than you do for yourself?

10. *Do you have difficulty thinking and acting as you would wish?* For example, do you feel that you must still meet an external standard? Do you watch your actions to make sure that you are behaving correctly? Do you worry excessively what others will think?

Total "Yes" answers (0-10) under Undeveloped Resilience _____

Paradoxical Resilience

To determine if you use your resilience paradoxically, ask yourself the following questions:

1. *Do you use your strengths and personal power in only one part of your life?* For example, do you limit the use of certain of your capacities only to work or only to your family; i.e., are you decisive at work, but not at home? Do you find you have more patience at work than at home? Or that you have more patience at home than at work?

2. *Do you feel you are two people, or have two selves, because you deal with challenges in different spheres of your life so differently?* For example, are you competent when dealing with personal decisions at work, but not at

home? Do you feel that you have a home demeanor and a work demeanor that are in contrast to each other, assertive in one place and passive in the other?

3. *Do you fear using your strengths and resourcefulness in your personal life?* For example, are you afraid that a loved one would leave you if he or she saw how capable you are? Do you fear that you must be appear weak and less than you are to keep a man in your life?

4. *Do you fear using your strengths and resourcefulness in your work life?* For example, do you fear that others will compete with you if they saw your abilities? Do you fear that others would be angry with you if you were more forthcoming? Do you fear that being more competent at work would prove to be a burden and overwhelm you?

5. *Do you feel burdened by somehow being more capable or competent or resourceful than others?* For example, do you fear that this will single you out as needing to perform better than others? Do you fear that more will be expected of you? Do you fear that somehow you will make yourself work harder if you own your competency?

6. *Are you afraid that your personal powers will drive others away from you, particularly those you need?* For example, are you concerned that you cannot be both competent and needy? Are you concerned that your capacities will prove to be frightening to another?

7. *Do you believe that luck determines many of your successes?* For example, do you feel that outcomes are not really within your control? Do you believe that luck played a large part in achieving them, and does this belief stop you from feeling pride in yourself?

8. *If you work hard on something, is it difficult for you to take credit for its success?* For example, do you feel you need to attribute success to others rather than owning it for yourself? Is it difficult to see your own personal power in making something happen?

9. *Do you worry about not having the ability to accomplish tasks that you have accomplished successfully in the past?* For example, do you lack confidence in yourself? Does this result in your becoming anxious or feeling dread as you approach a new task or challenge?

10. *Do you feel that you must appear weak, less than you are, in order to have people love you or be close to you?* For example, do you fear your strength will scare others away? Do you fear that you must be alone with your strengths, capacities, and desires because they will be unappreciated by another?

Total "Yes" answers (0-10) under Paradoxical Resilience _____

Self-Contained Resilience

To determine if you use your resilience in a self-contained way ask yourself:

1. *As a child, did you feel that you could only depend on yourself?* For example, did you feel that your only chance of survival was not to rely on someone else? Were you frequently disappointed by the adults around you?

2. *Was mastery of any threat the most important aspect of dealing with it—more important, for example, than being comforted?* For example, were you uncomfortable in allowing others to see that you were afraid as a child? Did you feel that you had to deal with problems alone? Did you focus your energies on conquering those issues in your life that were the most frightening?

3. *Do you still depend primarily or only on yourself?* Do you have problems trusting others? For example, do you keep an eye on those close to you to see if they are about to disappoint you? Do you feel that you must be ever vigilant?

4. *Are you impatient with others when their way of handling tasks differs from yours?* For example, do you find yourself

critical of others, particularly those you are closest to? When others say that you are critical, does this come as a surprise to you because you only have their best interest at heart?

5. *Do work and other commitments keep you from being available to friends and family?* For example, do you find yourself frequently late or declining fun invitations because of work commitments? Do you feel your work is close to being mastered if only you do this one next thing? Do you find yourself disappointing those you are the closest to? Does your work serve to isolate you?

6. *When you are upset, do you find yourself turning to your areas of competence to distract you from your feelings?* For example, do you find that you throw yourself into work when you are upset? Does work provide an emotional comfort? If everything else seems to be going poorly, do you feel at least you can control your work?

7. *Do you feel that if you "could" do something you "should" do it?* For example, do you find that you rely only on your competency to determine how you will approach something that needs to be done? Do you find that even if you do not want to do something, you do it anyway?

8. *Do you fail to factor in your desire to accomplish tasks along with your ability to do them?* For example, do you find that you do not listen to how you feel or how motivated you are in approaching a task, seeking merely to get it over with, whatever the personal cost? Do you fear being lazy if you postpone something that needs attention?

9. *Are you more comfortable with your competent self, rather than your needy self?* For example, do you find yourself spending more time trying to shine through accomplishments than trying to determine what you need and taking care of this part of you? Is it more comfortable to perform and earn what you need than to ask for it?

10. *Are you more comfortable producing something than feeling your feelings?* For example, do you switch into production gear when you are upset—bake a cake, pull out some paperwork, garden? Do you feel that figuring out what you need to do for yourself takes too much time from your work?

*Total "Yes" answers (0-10) under Self-Contained Resilience*_____

Overwhelmed Resilience

To determine if your resilience is overwhelmed, ask yourself:

1. *Do you focus on your pain, going over and over again the same sad memories?* For example, do you feel trapped by these memories? Do you feel exhausted by the pain and stress when these memories recur? Are you unable to stop thinking of them?

2. *Do you ever "wish you were dead" as a solution to new or existing problems?* For example, do you wish you could disappear in stressful moments? Do you wish the earth could swallow you and you would be gone?

3. *As a child did you ever wish you had never been born?* For example, was it so hard to be a child that you would frequently wish to disappear? Did you feel your birth was a mistake, one that you have paid for ever since? Did you feel that you or your family would have been much happier if you were never conceived?

4. *Do you have little or no access to your personal power?* For example, is it difficult to make decisions? Do you find it hard to know what it is that you need to do to take care of yourself? Do you feel more acted upon than active in your life?

5. *Do you deny or not know what you need?* For example, when someone asks what you need, do you draw a blank or switch the question to see what it is that they need? Does it feel almost impossible to reach this part of you?

6. *Do you feel shame when you think of your own neediness?* For example, is it shameful to be seen as needy? Are needs all right for others but not for you? Do you wish that you did not have any needs?

7. *Do you have periods of hating yourself?* For example, have you ever wanted to hurt yourself or kill yourself? Have you ever planned to hurt yourself as a punishment?

8. *Do you focus on caring for others as a way of avoiding caring for yourself?* For example, is it easier to see what others need than what you need? Does caring for others allow you to feel that at least you know how to do something right? Is caring for others the closest that you come to experiencing caring at all?

9. *Do you feel trapped by the past and unable to move beyond it?* For example, do you feel defined by your childhood experiences and unable as an adult to redefine yourself? If you feel you were a victim as a child, does this equate to being a victim as an adult?

10. *Do you feel scarred or tainted by the experiences you have had as a child and an adult?* For example, do you feel less than others because of these experiences? Do you hold your present relationships hostage to your past? Do you fear you will be rejected if others knew of what you have endured?

Total "Yes" answers (0-10) under Overwhelmed Resilience_____

Stellar Resilience

To determine your degree of stellar resilience ask yourself:

1. *Have you encountered tragedy or formidable barriers in your life?* For example, have you ever been sexually, physically or verbally abused? Have you lost a parent, close relative, or friend? Have you lost a limb or the functioning of a part of your body?

2. *Have you often wondered how you survived while others around you did not do nearly as well as you?* For example, did you have a sibling who became mentally ill or addicted? Did your friends get into difficulty with the law, turn to prostitution, or drop out of school? Did family members struggle with addiction, poverty, or disabilities?

3. *Are you actively working to create a better life than the one that you had as a child?* For example, do you try to make sure that there is enough good food to eat? If you experienced violence as a child, do you work to ensure a safe environment? If you experienced abuse, do you work to create a loving environment? If your childhood home was chaotic, do you strive to create an orderly and consistent environment?

4. *Do you struggle with the feeling that you do not know what a "normal" lifestyle is because you have never experienced what "normal" people have?* For example, do you feel at a loss as to how to conduct your life, because you have so little guidance from your childhood? Do you feel that you do not know how others live, how they manage, or how they have avoided the pain that you know all too well?

5. *Do you feel that you have a normal life now, but that it is a pretense because you really don't know the ground rules?* For example, do you feel that you get by in life by the seat of your pants, or that you can fail as easily as succeed because there is something everyone else knows that you don't? Do you fear being found out or rejected if others learn of your past? Do you feel that your lifestyle now is beyond what you dreamed of as a child but that it may be taken away from you?

6. *Do you feel you are not entitled to feel good or to come first if doing so means that someone you care for must come second?* For example, do you take care of everyone

else before you take care of yourself? Are you so sensitive to the needs of others that you forget that you have needs as well?

7. *Do you feel that your life is successful?* For example, are you proud of what you have accomplished? Do you feel that you have fashioned a life that suits you and makes sense for you? Have you accomplished some of the goals that you set for yourself?

8. *Do you feel a need to help others because you understand what it is to suffer?* For example, have you chosen a career in which your primary responsibility is the well-being of others, such as in teaching, medicine, or counseling? Do you volunteer your time in such areas?

9. *Do you, or did you, see yourself as wanting to save the world or one very special part of it?* For example, do you acutely feel the pain and suffering in the world and want to make it stop? Do you become angry, agitated, sad, hopeless, or depressed when hearing the news? Do you just avoid the news all together?

10. *Do you see yourself as a survivor?* For example, are you conscious of having made it through a difficult past and feel that you possess the ability to do this in your life? Do you think of yourself as essentially tough—either on the outside or inside?

Total "Yes" answers (0-10) under Stellar Resilience _____

Scoring Your Personal Profile

For each category, tally the number of positive responses.

- 7 to 10 "Yes" responses in a single category indicate a *major area* of resilience for you.
- 4 to 6 "Yes" responses in a single category indicate a *moderate area* of resilience for you.

- 0 to 3 "Yes" responses in a single category indicate a *low area* of resilience for you.

How to Use Your Resilience Profile

You can expect to find a major or moderate reading in more than one category. This resulting profile indicates your progression in the development of your resilience—where you began and where you are now. It can also highlight future areas in which you may want to concentrate. For example, you may find that you have most characteristics of stellar resilience because you have achieved many personal goals against great odds and have a need to help others overcome the difficulties you experienced, but in some ways you are somewhat too self-reliant and isolated, two common traits of those of self-contained resilience. This would indicate that you have been able to move beyond the earlier coping styles you used when you felt that you needed to do everything yourself, to a style that reflects your pride in knowing that you have survived and can now more freely interact with others. Further, you may see that you are reluctant to exercise your competence in certain areas, a sign of paradoxical resilience. You may decide that your occasional isolation is fine, but want to develop your resilience in all areas of your life, not just some. You will want to concentrate on the growth tasks of the paradoxically resilient.

Or you may find that your resilience may be described as balanced but that you experience shame concerning certain issues. This allows you to know that you have worked through being overwhelmed and are on your way to achieving a more balanced resilience. You may choose to work on shame as a way of elevating and integrating your overall pattern of resilience. Or you may find your resilience is basically balanced, but because of some childhood traumas, you have some stellar qualities. You may decide to use your resilience to explore more of your childhood and understand its impact on your adult life.

My experience has taught me that no matter the degree of resilience you have already developed, you can learn to recognize it more consciously and use it more effectively to get what you want and need. Remember, your resilience profile is composed of the coping skills you have developed to date. It highlights the struggle you have encountered in your life, describes how you have made sense of these, and can point you in a new direction of growth as you consolidate the gains you have made. When you learn to recognize your resilience, you can incorporate its guidance into your everyday life and know that it will aid you in times of greater stress and trial.

CHAPTER 4

Growing Up: The Lessons of Childhood

For most of us, childhood reminiscence is bittersweet. We have our favorite memories of special people, places, and events. Looking back to these memories is much like flipping through the pages of a familiar family photo album, where pictures capture the great and small events in those growing years.

This is not all of childhood, however. Imprinted as vividly in our memories are times of frustration, failures, temper tantrums, and tears. These, too, are a part of childhood and how we learned, struggling by trial and error until we developed our problem-solving skills. Often we forget that these memories are just as integral, just as much a part of who we are, as the happier moments.

To depict childhood as an idyllic and magical time, free from cares and woes, belies the intense efforts we as children exerted to master new skills, absorb losses and changes, and find our way. Portraying childhood as a time devoid of challenge is a particular disservice to women, for it reinforces society's stereotype of women as helpless and less capable. It tells us that our hard-won battles were frivolous or worse. As a result, we may be tempted to view our childhood years with dissatisfaction, even contempt, because they don't fit the ideal.

It may be difficult for us, then, to look back to this time in order to assimilate these diverse experiences. Yet our ability to use our resilience as a conscious force in our lives requires us to take such a look to understand the impact, both positive and negative, that our experiences had on us. We need to look at our family and see more realistically the lessons we learned and the values we were taught. Such a perspective will allow us to understand what belongs to us and us alone, and how we are separate and different from our family. In this way we can more surely find our own resilient voice.

This backward glance is valuable no matter what our pattern of resilience. This investigation can enable those with self-contained or paradoxical resilience to trace the influences on their resilience and see new options to increase their flexibility. Women of overwhelmed resilience can benefit from a new perspective that reinforces their ability to put aside old and damaging beliefs. Women of stellar resilience can gain a better understanding of their unique situation, which can help them learn to care for themselves even as they care for others. Finally, for all women who wish to strengthen their resilience, revisiting their childhood will give them an insight into the creative beginnings of their inner voice, which they can develop further.

In this chapter and the next, I encourage you to look again at your childhood experiences without judging how close to an ideal they came. Rather, appreciate what you learned and why you learned what you did. The lessons we learn in childhood have lasting consequences. What our family was and was not able to provide often holds the key to our adult resilience.

Origins of Resilience

Our first lessons in resilience come in childhood as we try to make sense of the world and find our place within it. We experiment with different ways of having our needs and desires met. We see how the adults in our lives, especially our parents, complete tasks and solve problems. We witness daily the manner in which they express love, face failure, and meet challenges.

As children we were practical. We came to conclusions concerning what worked best for us, what gave us the attention we needed, and what brought us rewards or helped us avoid pain. We learned the behaviors our parents reinforced and the behaviors they discouraged. We came to understand the consequences and efficiency of our actions by trial and error. Meaning and social considerations came later. Through this understanding we began to develop our own coping style.

The quest of every child is to find a positive self-image. We want to see ourselves as powerful, competent, and influential beings, worthy of love and regard. Our innate programming propels us toward mastery in physical, mental, and social development. If our homes were warm and nurturing, our parents and other adults helped us achieve these positive goals and reinforced our efforts toward them. We learned to trust ourselves because our parents trusted us first. We learned to love ourselves through their love of us. Children from such families internalize the insight, compassion, and self-regard they experience from loving caretakers.

I recently watched as a small girl of five came running to her mother crying on the first day of soccer practice.

"I can't do it!" she cried. "It's too hard."

Her mother scanned the crowd of parents, aware that her daughter was the only child who was giving up just as she had begun.

"It's all right, Elyssa," her mother said calmly. "It may seem hard right now, but I know you can do it. You're a good, fast runner. You can do fine."

Minutes later Elyssa once more came crying to her mother's side. Again her mother reassured her, "You can do it. I know you can. Yes, it is hard, but you've done other hard things and you can do this. Remember swimming? It seemed hard at first, too, but after a while it was your favorite. It might be the same with soccer, but you need to try."

Head bowed, Elyssa returned once more to the field, moving slowly, then running. In a few minutes she had taken her place among the other girls and boys, obviously enjoying herself and delighting in her speed and skill as a runner.

Elyssa's mother is a powerful woman, I thought; she is such a good teacher. Later I wondered that if I had told her so, if she would have dismissed it, saying, "Oh, well, I was just doing my job," or, "I'm not powerful; I was just helping my daughter." She would probably not see as I did that such everyday responses of a mother to her child represent vital lessons in resilience, the value of which extends far beyond simply learning a new skill or overcoming fear of new situations. In these simple interactions, Elyssa's mother taught her daughter several important lessons about herself and her abilities.

First, her mother reassured Elyssa that she could do well in this new sport. It might seem hard, but she could handle difficult moments. Her mother's reminder that she had faced other new situations and mastered other skills helped Elyssa remember these successes and draw confidence from them.

Elyssa's mother acknowledged and validated her daughter's feeling of being overwhelmed even while she encouraged Elyssa to remember that she had other qualities on which she could concentrate instead, such as her skill as a runner. She was larger than the part that felt overwhelmed. Her mother helped Elyssa see herself from a different perspective and discover new options. Rather than acting on the first choice that came to her—to give up—Elyssa could choose another response—to try again. By not insisting that Elyssa return to practice but giving her the choice, her mother reinforced her daughter's sense of control over the situation. In later years, Elyssa will likely be able to draw upon her various resilient qualities in meeting life's challenges.

A Difficult Childhood

Not all children are so fortunate, however. Instead, their childhood experiences were stressful or abusive. They had no one to provide the consistent guidance and support other children receive. Yet many disadvantaged and high-risk children nevertheless learn these lessons as well or better than their luckier counterparts. In many respects, it is a paradox: on the one hand, children from disadvantaged homes are vulnerable to their parents' inadequate nurturing; while on the other, they are challenged to learn to care for themselves. To a degree, the more stress on the child, the more necessity and opportunity exist for the child to compensate through experimentation, learning to act on his or her own behalf, and developing new avenues for learning and support. The need to be self-sufficient often leads to high levels of functioning in such individuals.

When I think of resilience in this context, I am reminded of Susan, a classmate of mine. Her father was a violent alcoholic who periodically would come intoxicated to school to yell at her or the principal or our teacher for some real or imagined wrong. Sometimes there were bruises on Susan's face and legs, which we all pretended not to see. She had a younger sister and brother for whom she was often responsible.

None of this stopped her from being the top student in our class. When her mother came home from work, Susan walked to the library to do her homework, after she had straightened the house and cooked dinner. Sometimes Susan went to a friend's house to do homework. Later as I got to know her, she came to mine.

I asked Susan once how she managed to do all she did. She told me how desperately she wanted to get out of her family's lifestyle, and she knew school was her only chance. She said she felt different from the rest of her family because she saw herself as a survivor. She concentrated on fulfilling this self-image. As years passed, I heard news of Susan, of the advanced degrees she earned and her career as a state legislator. Susan's clear vision and determination were all part of her resilience.

It is important to stress that there is a limit to the positive outcomes of such a challenge on young children. In their need to achieve competence in certain areas, children are often forced to neglect other areas of development, such as the ability to form lasting relationships and express needs. Without protective factors that can allow children to moderate hard-won coping strategies, they are at risk of developing an unbalanced style of resilience.

What We Needed: Protection and Independence

Children need many things from their parents and other caregivers. Of these, protection and independence are particularly significant in the development of resilience. A child must have appropriate measures of each, although they can be conflicting and confusing at times, even overwhelming, for parents and child alike.

The conflict between protection and independence is evident in the two-year-old who wants to do it herself, yet cries if her mother walks out of the room. It is equally present in the adolescent who complains that she is too restricted, not allowed to make her own decisions, but anxiously asks for her mother's opinion and support. The two needs represent a vital dynamic that shapes who we are, both as children and adults. Much depends on our ability to successfully achieve a healthy balance between them.

Protection

All children need protection. Learning safe behavior is a life-long process. But how is that protection to be given? The answer to this can make all the difference.

Imagine a one-year-old child coming into a room that has been made childproof. The child is able to explore without restrictions, to learn about the room and the objects in it, and about herself in relationship to them. The child can move independently and rove about as she wishes. If the room were not childproof, she could be protected by being held by her mother or being placed in a playpen. She would be equally safe but restricted and not free to be stimulated in the same way.

The degree to which a child should be protected is a constant consideration for parents. While it may be true that the "burned hand teaches best," parents must decide what is an acceptable risk and what is not. A mother must let her child learn to walk on her own and accept the many falls and tears along the way. Yet other situations are not so clear cut, and as the child grows, these situations become more and more a matter of individual judgment.

Learning how to protect herself is important for the child, because as soon as she begins to move around in her environment, she receives specific instructions that clearly imply that the world is not always safe. These range from warnings about safety hazards—a hot stove or busy street—to rules for her social behavior, such as not taking candy from strangers, not letting anyone touch her in a certain way, and so forth.

Parents can teach these lessons in various ways. Unfortunately, many parents instill a sense of fear or shame as a way to teach their children appropriate behavior. For a healthy balance, children need to learn to protect themselves not out of fear, but out of respect for themselves and their bodies so they can demand that others respect them also.

I was at a mall during the holiday season one year and had an opportunity to observe two mother-daughter interactions. In the first instance, a frustrated mother, her arms full of packages, yanked her four-year-old daughter's coat in an effort to move the dawdling girl along. Her daughter yelled at her, "Stop it! You're hurting me!" The mother stopped. Still frustrated, but also visibly upset, she said, "I'm sorry, I didn't mean to hurt you, but we have to get going!"

Shortly after this I observed another mother and daughter. Again the mother, burdened by too many packages, was trying to make her way through the crowds with her five-year-old daughter. The girl stopped at a toy counter to look at the dolls. Her mother turned angrily to her and smacked her across her back. The girl didn't say anything. She hung her head and followed her mother out of the store. This interaction led me to suspect a very different relationship between mother and daughter. Here the child was being raised to believe that being hit was acceptable, and her hung head seemed to say that she knew she was to blame.

These mother-daughter pairs had much in common. Both girls were well dressed and well groomed. Both had the attention of their mother in this very busy mall. But the quality of their attention varied greatly. The first girl had received a yank from her mother, but also her mother's acknowledgment that this was wrong behavior. Already by age four, the daughter felt entitled to articulate her feelings and to stand up for herself, even against her mother. The second girl had learned not to stand up to her mother, outwardly at least. She learned it was acceptable for parents to hit children and that it was her fault if she were hit. I thought about what very different lessons each mother taught her daughter about self-protection and her right to be treated with respect.

Independence

While children need protection, they have an equal and ever-increasing need for independence from family and home. Independence means moving away from parents, out of their protection. Many parents find it difficult to accept that as their daughter matures, they become increasingly less central to her accomplishments and developing sense of self. Yet it is important that parents support and facilitate her desire to act for herself and make her own decisions.

A child growing up with a good sense of independence knows that she has her parent's trust. Whether independence means spending her first night at a friend's house or cooking her first meal, a girl nurtured in her independence feels her family's support, even if she cries at her friend's house and needs to come home, even if her first meal is inedible. To try is to learn and to grow. With each success her self-esteem grows a little more, and she is more prepared to assume responsibility for her actions and their consequences.

Just when to allow a child greater independence and how much to allow is a cause for parents' concern. A young child will let her parents know that she is ready for a new challenge by her increasing ability to handle new situations and her growing interest in these new skills. As a child becomes older, the cues to her need for independence are different. Even when she can say, "I can do it," a parent needs to judge whether in fact she can.

Achieving a Balance

A good balance between decreasing protection and increasing independence is very important to a girl's healthy development. One who is overprotected and not allowed to make mistakes may conclude that she is incompetent or that she can only have what she wants if others obtain it for her. As an adult, she is liable to have an underdeveloped resilience. She will continue to look for protection from others, such as her spouse, her boss, a more experienced co-worker, or a mentor.

Appropriate independence is also very different from too much independence. While it is true that some children are able to cope with too much independence and go on to assume a stellar resilience, they do so at a cost to their inner well being. More often, girls who are given little protection and too much independence develop feelings of shame when they confront situations for which they are unequipped. Unable to judge how much is appropriate for themselves at that age, they believe they are to blame when they are asked to do too much or when they need more adult help. This often sets the stage for over-whelmed resilience. Or a child may develop a self-contained resilience style, feeling that she must keep achieving, because that is all of who she is and she has no other choice.

Many years ago I counseled a mother and daughter during the girl's spring break from an exclusive boarding school. Ostensibly, they came to see me about the intense arguments they were having about how much money the daughter would receive each month when she went to spend the summer by herself in New York City. Crystal was only fourteen years old. When I expressed my amazement that such a young girl would be allowed to live on her own in New York City, her mother hastened to assure me that Crystal would only be subletting a friend's apartment in a very fashionable part of Manhattan and that her daughter was looking forward to beginning her modeling career. "We have family in the city, so if anything happens, Crystal will have people to call."

"Where will you be?" I asked the mother.

"I'll be in Europe with my fiancé."

It was clear that the arguing was not about money but the fact that Crystal was terrified about being on her own in the city, even though she was loathe to admit to it. She found it easier to sabotage the whole plan by getting her mother angry than to admit she couldn't handle so much freedom. We reached a compromise: Crystal agreed to stay with relatives and not sublet an apartment. The money issue evaporated.

Situations such as Crystal's may put a girl at risk of developing a paradoxical resilience. Unable to ask for help or to admit that what is expected of her is more than she can master, she may compartmental-ize her skills, developing strengths in her chosen career, but remaining overwhelmed and unable to access her resilience in other areas of her life. She may have a difficult time in seeing her strengths outside of a work environment, for example. If Crystal were to pursue modeling, her looks may become so important that she may feel that her beauty is the only reason she is of value. She will need help understanding how to express her needs and how to nurture herself in many different ways rather than focusing so much of her identity on one aspect of herself.

My Own Protection and Independence

Give yourself some time to relax and think about the following questions. Ask your resilient voice to help you answer them.

- Did your parents understand what you needed to feel safe?
- Did they readily provide this, or were they angered or overwhelmed by your needs? What did you learn from this about how to take care of yourself?
- Did you feel that you were adequately protected as a child? Or did you feel it was up to you to provide the protection you needed? If so, how did you protect yourself?
- When you felt you were in danger, did your parents understand your feelings of vulnerability? Or did they make it clear that your feelings were not acceptable? What did you conclude about your need for protection?
- Did your vulnerabilities become the center of attention because they made your parents feel all the more needed? How do you make sense of this as an adult?
- Are you comfortable now asking for the assistance you need, or do you feel you must be self-sufficient? Is it shameful to be needy? Are you unable to ask?
- Were you encouraged to believe that the world was a dangerous place and you should not venture into it? How does this affect you today?
- Did you feel overprotected? Could you not move beyond your parents' purview without hurting their feelings? Does this still shape your responses to them and perhaps other authority figures?

- Looking back, did you feel crippled by your lack of experience in making decisions? How did you counter this in your childhood and adulthood?

- Were your needs for independence understood? If they were at one time but not another, note this. If they involved certain areas of life (relationships, school, hobbies) and not others, note this. How did you learn to compensate for this?

- Was too much expected of you too early? Were you allowed to say so, or was there no alternative other than to learn how to function on your own?

- Now when independent action is needed are you usually ready for it? Or do you feel overwhelmed or not capable? Do you feel that you must know what to do or else?

- Do you enjoy a sense of accomplishment from your efforts, or do they always seem insufficient or ineffective? Or are they too much and too isolating?

Now consider your resilience type. Can you begin to see how your early experiences in protection and independence shaped your resilience? Are there certain issues in these areas you see that could benefit from more attention?

Spend time with your resilient voice about these issues and how they influence your life as an adult.

Distress and Trauma

Providing a sound balance of protection and independence is difficult enough for a healthy family, but for a family experiencing chronic or extraordinary problems, the task of providing this balance for children can become a strain on an already overburdened family.

It is important to remember that all families have problems. Healthy families work productively to find solutions, obtaining outside help if necessary. Even during difficult times, they will continue to provide needed love and support for their members. In fact, working through manageable problems is a positive lesson that serves to bolster a family's strengths. An unhealthy family, by contrast, may be overwhelmed and even disintegrate in the face of difficulties.

For children, change and its resultant stress are a normal part of life: the first day of school, a theater tryout, or the first night away from home. Such distress may be uncomfortable, but often it propels us to new learning. The frustration of reaching for objects we could not yet grasp led us to stand and then to walk. It is part of developing a larger understanding of the world and gives us experience in responding to stresses and distressful events in life. We learn that most upsetting events are temporary and soon lose their importance. We learn to keep our disappointments in perspective and go on. These are valuable lessons that we can draw from in the future.

Trauma is very different from distress. Trauma is an abnormal life experience. Within a family, it might include sexual or physical abuse; the death of a parent or sibling; extreme poverty; divorce; alcoholic, addicted, or mentally ill parents; or intense fighting between family members. Disaster outside the family, such as a natural disaster, war, or tragedy, can be a source of trauma also.

When a child experiences unmitigated trauma, she may develop painful feelings about herself that are likely to be long lasting. These feelings do not disappear when the trauma is over, but form a basis of negative feelings about herself, perhaps worthlessness, unlovability, helplessness, or shame. Resolving trauma and its aftermath can be a long process, one very different from resolving distress.

Protective Factors: The Key to Resilience

Our ability to handle distress and trauma varies from one person to the next. Certain protective factors may provide us with the resilience to handle these situations and recover from their negative effects. Such factors include our unique attributes, our family environment, and the influence of the larger community.

Personal Attributes

Certain qualities in a person's physical and psychological makeup can form the basis of early resilience. Susan's initiative, for example, in finding ways to complete her homework, as well as her reliance on her own capabilities to build a better life for herself, arose from an inner sense of self she established early in life. This independent self-image allowed her to conceive of a different way of living than the one her family showed her. As a result, she was able to create a healthy distance between herself and the trauma of her father's alcoholism and chaotic home.

Family Environment

Our personal traits do not exist in a vacuum, but in the context of our family, which can contribute significantly to the development of our resilience or thwart it. Protective factors associated with families include family cohesiveness and the attention we receive from our parents, siblings, and other family members. The amount of structure and limit-setting provided in the home, especially during adolescence, are also variables.

While a family cannot protect a child completely from circumstances beyond its control, parents can mitigate the damaging effects of trauma. Positive features can play a crucial role in determining how those circumstances ultimately affect the child's later life.

Isabelle, a friend of mine, grew up in a Displaced Persons camp, one of hundreds of camps set up throughout Europe after World War II. Here homeless, war-torn families were reunited and struggled to reestablish their lives in the midst of chaos, poverty, and illness. When Isabelle talks of her childhood, she remembers her life in the camps as a time when she learned from her mother a sense of personal power.

By the age of five, Isabelle had learned to bargain for bread and get it at a price the family could afford. Survival skills, she explained, were well rewarded by her mother, and young Isabelle felt pride in her accomplishments, despite the stressful circumstances. These early achievements laid the foundation for subsequent successes in her life. As an adult today, Isabelle is a competent woman with a rewarding family life and professional career. She radiates fulfillment and warmth.

Ruth grew up in similar circumstances. She, however, looks back in horror at her life in the Displaced Persons camp. Ruth remembers the confusion, deprivation, and scant provisions. She remembers that her mother would curse her for being born, saying how much easier it would have been to feed a family of two rather than three. Ruth grew up feeling unwanted and as if there were nothing she could do to make life better. The lesson of her childhood was learning to endure—endure her mother's rages, the poverty, her own fears. Ruth grew up feeling less worthy than other children.

As an adult, Ruth continues to perceive herself this way. She faces life with determination but little spirit or self-esteem. She has worked for a large corporation since her graduation from college, moving up the corporate ladder in carefully defined steps. But in her personal life she is unhappy. She feels empty and has been unable to find fulfillment in a series of marriages. Her sadness is, in part, the pain of the familiar, the sense of despair and inadequacy she has carried with her all these years. It is also the pain of her own lack of vision that life could be different.

Community Environment

Just as the family can foster resilience and a child's healthy self-esteem, so the community can serve an important function in protecting a child. Within the caregiving environment outside the family, in the community as a whole, children benefit from dependable caretakers, supportive role models, and other social support.

Inez grew up in a poor family in Fresno, California. Her family was from Mexico and spoke Spanish at home. Inez taught herself English, first on the streets and later at school. Her father was disabled and her mother did domestic work. For most of her childhood, Inez, as the eldest child, functioned as the person in charge during her mother's absence.

"The brief exceptions were two weeks every summer when I was sent to the church-sponsored summer camp," said Inez. "When family friends told my mother about the camp, she at once made arrangements for me to go. I remember telling my mother that I didn't want to go, but she insisted that I have the chance to be a child, if only for a little while."

She remembers how difficult it was to leave her responsibilities: "I worried about my father and the rest of the kids. The first week I was pretty tense, but after that I began to relax and just be a kid. I'd play and swim. I remember the sense of freedom that I had. There were meals I didn't have to cook, friends I could just play with, and new things to learn, like ceramics. The counselors were wonderful. Every summer for seven years, I fell in love with my group leader. Some of them kept in touch with me over the years. Everything about camp made me feel special."

For Inez, summer camp was a different world, a place in which she could try on new roles and new ways of being. Her mother realized the value of giving her daughter exposure to different people and different lifestyles. It allowed Inez to dream. The lasting bond with adults in authority whom she knew on a first-name basis became the model on which Inez eventually built her own life. Today she is a teacher in the neighborhood in which she grew up. To all who know her, she is a walking success story.

Each woman develops her resilience to a different degree, depending on her unique experiences and the presence of risk and protective factors in her life. Even in the same family, siblings discover different ways of coping with their situation. Some people, for whatever reason, have low resilience; an imbalance between trauma and protective factors has not allowed them as yet to develop their natural resilience. Others regularly rely on their resilience to meet daily challenges. I frequently find that even people unaware of their resilience can nevertheless identify elements in their childhood from which they drew special strength and meaning.

Determining Your Own Protective Factors

Take a moment to ask yourself the following questions. Then write out your answers in two, three, or more sentences.

Which of the following protective factors, if any, were true of your situation growing up? What positive circumstances had a lasting effect on your life?

Individual Factors

- good health
- good problem-solving and communication skills
- self-esteem
- sense of control in one's life
- achievement orientation
- flexibility
- sense of humor
- empathy
- other

Family Factors

- strong family ties
- close, positive relationship with parent(s)
- nurturing extended family
- warm, caring, and supportive environment
- clear boundaries or set limits
- structure and consistency
- other

Community Factors

- positive school experiences
- positive religious affiliation
- close relationship(s)
- supportive role models
- group opportunities (camp, youth groups)
- consistent child care
- other

Which of these protective factors (or their equivalent) are present in your life today?

_____

Of Roots and Wings

As our resilience forms and develops under the influences of these early years, the stages through which we pass enable us to formulate two formidable components of our resilience: a knowledge of who we are—our *roots*—and a widening capacity to reach beyond our immediate situation to the wider world—our *wings*.

Our roots comprise the deep sense of self that arises from our interactions with the world, the responses we receive from our environment, and our increasing ability to obtain what we need. Even as infants, when we felt distress and needed comfort, our developing resilience allowed us to explore our bodies and to keep searching until we found our mouth and our thumb so that we could suck and soothe ourselves.

Our rootedness is our belief in that self, our determination to overcome whatever is placed in our path to get to where we need to go. This began with the long, determined process it took to learn our earliest skills—to sit, to crawl, to walk—and includes the mastery we now exercise in our everyday lives.

Our rootedness then is our identity that grows slowly over the years and results in our self-concept, what we know about ourselves. It is through this knowledge that we assess our strengths, weaknesses, and emerging capabilities. This is the part of us that contains our beliefs about who we are and retains our personal values.

Annalee, born in Vietnam, was adopted by American parents when she was six months old. Her birth mother had put her child up for adoption because she knew that Annalee, as the daughter of a young Vietnamese bar hostess and an African American serviceman, would be condemned to a life of discrimination in Vietnam.

Annalee's adoptive parents, a middle-class couple of Swedish and Finnish descent, lived in Minneapolis, Minnesota. They loved their little daughter with the passion known only to those who have gone childless and now finally have a baby to love.

"My parents saw themselves as a family now connected to Vietnam and the black community in America," said Annalee. "They made it a point to learn about Vietnam and to speak to me about it, so that the country of my birth was meaningful to me. My adoptive father had also been in the armed services, so he was able to talk about what life was probably like for my birth father."

As a family they became involved in cultural events that allowed them all to celebrate her heritage and theirs. This allowed Annalee to build a special sense of identity in which she took pride. This sustained her in dealing with the racism of the American culture.

Annalee also grew up on stories of how she was a sweet but determined baby, how she would focus her attention on a goal and keep on trying until she got achieved it. Whether she was tying her shoe or learning to read, her concentration was exemplary. This led to her being proud of her academic ability and developing pride in herself.

Annalee said, "I grew up knowing I was different from most kids around me, but as I got older, I liked my specialness. I realized that I had relatives in three countries that spoke languages other than English. So I began to study languages in elementary school. I gave up trying to be just like the other kids. I realized there was nothing I could do that would ever make me like them, so I decided to be the most me I could be.

"This was a long, hard struggle. I remember when I was about to have a solo in my third-grade Christmas show. I overheard two of my classmates saying that 'brown-skinned girls with slanty eyes can't sing.' I just dissolved into tears, and slumped to the floor. My mother wandered backstage and found me. She looked at me and held me. She always seemed to understand my pain, and she was pretty good at teaching me to fight back.

"After I finished a good hard cry she said, 'Let's go show them how truly ignorant they are.' I belted out 'Santa Claus Is Coming to Town' as it had never been sung before!"

Today Annalee in college on a scholarship, majoring in French and Vietnamese. Annalee said, "I'm happy that I know and like who I am. I enjoy playing up my individuality."

Our roots give us a valuable connection to our past and the positive experiences that helped to make us who we are. Here, in our roots, are the bumps we encountered that set us on a new direction, the molds we used only to recast later on. Here is our past which exerts its influence on our present.

Our Wings

Our wings provide us with another aspect of our resilience that is very different from our roots. While our rootedness stems from the depths of our being, our wings enable us to extend our vision beyond our experience to reach out into the world. Our wings allow us to use our fantasies for practical purposes.

We were developing our wings when we spent our time as children in imaginary play, writing stories or reading of other worlds, princesses, and happy endings. We met people with other lives and imagined ourselves to be them. It was through such dreaming that we began to know more about the world, to sense our own desires for the future. We learned a bit about what life had to offer, and we began to glimpse what we wanted for ourselves. We even used our wings to help shape the life we wanted to have.

Julia was born into a working-class family of five children. Her father was a fireman and a chronic gambler who lost most of his paycheck each month. Her mother, unable to get by on her husband's earnings, was dependent on her own family for food and small loans. Even as a young child, Julia saw how indebted her mother was to her grandmother.

"With that kind of power over my mother, my grandmother exacted a heavy price in the form of obedience to her every whim. I never wanted to be so beholden to someone else," said Julia.

She vowed as a young child not to get married, not to be poor, not to be so helplessly trapped as her mother was. Julia began to dream of other lives. She fell in love with movies and television and the different characters she saw there. Julia said, "I spent hours fantasizing about the people and the lives they lived. I remember I drove my family crazy trying to speak like the characters so I could lose my Bronx accent. My brothers told me I was showing off. But my playacting allowed me to imagine that my life could be different and better than my parents'."

Another favorite pastime was to go with her father to the Bronx zoo, not just to see the animals, but to speak to the people who worked there about their jobs and about how they knew that they wanted to work in a zoo. She asked the same questions of the nuns who taught her. "I was always told I was such a curious child," said Julia. "Maybe I was just nosy, but I wanted to know how people got to where I saw them in life. I always felt that life wasn't something that happened to you, it was something that you went out and found."

Early on, Julia used her natural inquisitiveness and interest in people to find out how she could make her life into what she intuitively knew she wanted. Today Julia is in an executive training program in personnel for a large hotel chain. Her natural inquisitiveness and eagerness to go out and learn about people has paid off.

To their credit, her parents supported Julia's interests as well as they could. "Although my mother didn't understand me," said Julia, "she also didn't try to stop my dreaming. She, too, had dreams of a better life for us, but she wasn't sure what that would mean. And my father, the gambler and ultimate dreamer, in a funny way fed my fantasies. After a trip to the zoo or a museum, he'd ask at the dinner table where my brothers and sister could hear, 'And what did you learn today about being a zookeeper, or a museum guard, or a subway attendant?' He found my answers amusing, and that gave me a permission to continue, no matter what my brothers thought."

Now that we are adults, our wings still allow us to imagine a different life, to continue to dream, just as we did as little girls. Our dreams and fantasies are a central part of who we are. Sometimes we share our dreams with friends or family and invite their assistance in making these dreams become reality. Or we may keep our dreams private and use them ourselves to help us develop a clearer image of who we are and what we can become.

Discovering Our Past

In childhood and adolescence we are often unaware of the quality of our upbringing or the full meaning of our early influences. Our attention is so focused on the challenges of new discovery and development just ahead of us, we don't take time to look back. We may not recognize the unique blend of our parents' strengths and shortcomings and how they affected our ability to develop our roots and wings.

In later years, however, we begin to see the significance of these influences. Sometimes the consequences of the ways in which our parents protected us or gave us their permission to grow may not be evident until we are parents ourselves, making the same decisions for our children. We may experience the same difficulty as our parents in achieving a healthy balance. Or we may need to live apart from our family for some time before we recognize how deep our roots or how wide our wings have grown.

In developing our resilience, we can begin to discover the benefits and failings of the past. We can draw on past strengths to make us stronger, or work through past traumas to make us more of who we want to be.

CHAPTER 5

Family Legacies

We receive nourishment for our growing resilience, our roots and our wings, from many sources. These include our personal encounters with the world, as well as what we learn from others, especially our family. Among our most important lessons are those our relatives teach us about life, about ourselves, and about how to make our way in the world. These lessons define our family's values, ingrained beliefs, attitudes, and lifestyle. A family's main teaching vehicle is its stories.

Our Family's Tales

Virtually every family has its well-worn tales. These stories involve parents, grandparents, and assorted relatives, real or fictionalized. They speak of how our relatives set out to meet their destiny and describe what they encountered along the way. In anecdotes and yarns, we learn of the rogues and scoundrels, the heroes and the saints, that abound in each family.

These stories teach us what life is all about; we learn that life is hard or fun, unfair or not to be taken too seriously. As young children listening to these tales, we form our vision of the future. If this vision is positive, we have permission to soar, to equal or better past triumphs. If the vision is negative, we may feel our options are limited, or we may experience more difficulty separating from our family.

Stories frequently function as parables or fables, offering conclusions and morals. We learn by their example about good choices and the consequences of not following rules or traditions. We learn what constitutes success, how to deal with failure, and how dreams can come true. Sometimes these are tales that tell us what ancestors learned or what they wished they had done.

Life Rafts

The eminent psychologist Bruno Bettelheim spoke of family stories as potential life rafts, passed down from one generation to the next. Indeed, some stories buoy us above our current circumstances and allow us to glimpse the strength, courage, tenacity, or cleverness used by our ancestors to overcome adversity. The significance of these stories lies not in their facts, but in the messages or meanings they convey. In our darkest moments, such stories remind us that others have traveled this way before us, confronting trials as great as those we now face. We are not as alone as we thought.

A friend told me a story concerning her ancestor Yung Mee. This ancestor was married to a rice farmer in South Korea more than two hundred years ago. Yung Mee's husband was the oldest son in his family and her responsibility, as his wife, was to observe the Lunar New Year. This ritual involves preparing special foods and arranging them in a particular order for a family feast. The whole family then gathers and hopes the spirits of their departed relatives will join them in the feast.

One year it seemed unlikely that Yung Mee would be able to keep this holiday. She had just given birth to twins and was still recuperating as the day approached. Nevertheless, she issued the invitation for all to attend. Her husband's family arrived skeptical, concerned that this most important holiday would not be properly observed. Instead they found the delicious feast perfectly arranged. When asked how she had done this, Yung Mee demurely smiled. It was said that her deceased in-laws themselves had come to help her prepare the feast.

"As a little girl, hearing this story," my friend said, "I was very literal. I wanted to know just how Yung Mee had done this. Who had really helped her? My grandmother smiled at my insistence. That was the point of the story, grandmother told me. We don't know. We cannot know—just as we cannot always know how we will accomplish what seems to be impossible for us. The story of Yung Mee tells us to go ahead anyway, for a way will be found."

The importance for the family repeating this tale is the message that miracles are possible when one does what is right. The degree of literal truth in this story does not matter. This tale and others like it supported this family during the Korean war and their later immigration to America. Yung Mee's faith and resolution when called upon to do the impossible made the family's hardships bearable and somehow understandable. "Remember Yung Mee," they would say, meaning "miracles are possible."

Handed down from generation to generation, these stories define us as a family and give us a sense of identity, our roots. Our family's teaching stories tell us how people in our family are supposed to act and the values to be upheld: family first; the importance of money, honesty, and hard work; individual freedom. They spell out our family's beliefs: when things get difficult, you need to try harder; women are usually wrong; stay with what you know. When taken together, these themes make up the characteristics that define our family as special and unique. These narratives are subtly shaped by each generation's viewpoint and often refashioned from one telling to the next.

Our Own Legacy: Our Roots and Wings

Through our family's stories we can discover personal meanings that bear on our developing resilience. Our family's oral history enables us to develop a sense of who we are, a sense of connectedness with others that can allow us to feel less isolated, more empowered, and better able to meet the challenges that lie before us. These stories allow us to say, "I come from a family of immigrants, risk-takers, adventurers, farmers, or professionals." This identity can feed our resilience by reinforcing our roots.

"I come from a family with strong women and a clear sense of right and wrong," Cheryl told me. "My mother was deeply religious, and the solace she received from her faith carried us through many difficult times. My mother taught Bible studies in our church. My love of Bible study taught me to love school and made me realize that learning was what I did best.

"I grew up in poverty on a farm in rural Georgia. None of my kinfolk went to school beyond sixth grade. But I had a dream and I knew I came from a family that makes dreams a reality. There was my great-great-grandfather, a freed slave, who wanted to own some land. He worked hard, very hard, for years until he could buy a few acres. My grandmother, too, wanted something impossible. She wanted to play the organ. Our family tells how she would come up with all sorts of ways of making small amounts of money, which she saved to pay for her lessons.

"So I wanted to be a teacher. I wanted to complete high school and go to college. I've made that dream come true. Like my forebears I, too, developed a plan and worked hard until I achieved my goal."

Through our family's oral history we, like Cheryl, can develop an understanding of who we are and the forces that formed our beliefs. They define our strengths as they give us roots.

Stories can also fill us with visions beyond our daily life. They nourish our wings, our dreams for ourselves. Even when we look at our circumstances and see only chaos and pain in our immediate surroundings, stories can tell us of larger vistas and new possibilities. Patricia, now a successful professional, told me of her childhood.

Patricia said, "When I was a girl, living in a home characterized by violence, abuse, and alcoholism, I blamed my mother for many things that were wrong with my life. I saw her weakness, her confusion, anger, and self-centeredness. I've since come to see that, vulnerable and weak as she was, my mother in fact gave me many gifts of value, although I did not consciously recognize them as such at the time.

"Those gifts were my mother's stories. She would tell us tales, largely fanciful, of the heroic exploits of our relatives who challenged life as they saw it and created change. My favorite story is one she told me in response to my asking about our heritage. In actuality, my mother is Ukrainian and my father Irish, but instead of telling me this, she told me that we were related to Cherokee Indians. She created a legend of a great-great-grandfather who came to America, married a Cherokee, and took her back to Ukraine. 'This is where you get your dark hair,' she told me.

"I was only eight years old," Patricia said. "I believed this story and felt connected to the Cherokee, a heritage that was more available and more positive than my troubled immediate family. I began to think of myself as Cherokee. I would braid my hair, wear headbands, and run like the wind. I felt proud, strong. I felt a part of something larger than myself from which I could draw strength. It fed my deepest conviction that I was different, special in a way that my day-to-day life belied, and that one day I would live up to this great promise."

Today Patricia recognizes those stories as the gifts they were. "It was as though on some level my mother realized that she could not do much to change what was happening within my family, but she gave me what she could," said Patricia. By encouraging her daughter's use of fantasy Patricia's mother gave her permission to dream. This allowed Patricia to look past the immediate confusion and pain and envision how different life could be.

"It didn't matter that these stories of my ancestry had no basis in historical fact," said Patricia. "On some level I knew they contained an important truth. They told me I was special, that I had inner, untried qualities I could learn to draw on. In that respect, they were absolutely true.

"Looking back, I'm not sure how much my mother herself recognized this inner meaning, but it may be that she did. For my own part, I am amazed that my eight-year-old self could understand this aspect of my mother's stories and instinctively derive such strength from it."

Patricia's resilience was in evidence even then, allowing her to see the light and nurturing aspects of an otherwise dark childhood. Through this recognition, Patricia has been able to make peace with her mother and come to terms with her past.

"Best of all," she said, "this understanding has enabled me to be the mother I want to be to my children."

Stories About Us

Of all the stories we hear from our family, the most essential to our early identity are those about ourselves. Their unspoken meanings and the ways in which they are told give us evidence of how we were viewed as a child. If our family jokingly speaks of our insatiable appetite and how quickly we grew, it implies that we were loved and that we challenged our family even as an infant. We may find these same themes repeated in later stories about ourselves, how we challenged our teachers, how we read earlier than others in our class, or how we asked questions that were difficult to answer. These stories form images that help us establish an identity. We feel good about ourselves.

Yet if the same story of our appetite is told to emphasize how demanding we were, how selfish and disrespectful we were of other's needs, or how we were never satisfied even as a breast-feeding infant, it gives us a very different feeling about ourselves. We learn that we were difficult, abnormal, and somewhat out of control. We were a problem for our parents. A story told in this manner has the potential to produce shame. Stories with this theme told throughout childhood can make us feel bad about ourselves, especially if the theme reverberates with other stories of our being difficult or being a burden to caretakers.

The effects of such a characterization may continue to be detrimental even as we grow to adulthood. These stories may be a way for family members to shame us, detract from our adult status, and keep us in a familiar, one-down role. Our present identity within the family may tie us to events long past—mistakes, for example that we are powerless to rectify. If we let them, stories can serve to keep us small and dependent and lead us to think poorly of ourselves. These constitute the dark legacies we may need to change.

Stories about Me

Think for a moment about stories you heard about yourself as a child. Allow your resilient voice to answer as you ask yourself what these stories told you. Write out your answers for future reference.

What did these stories tell you
- about yourself?
- about your relationship with your parents?
- about your place in the family?

Are these stories reflective of you as an adult? Do you feel that they are accurate about the person you were as a child?

Is it possible to separate stories about you from your parents' reactions to you?

Developing Female Traditions

Our family's tales about our women relatives hold a special importance for us as women. They reveal the strategies, successful and otherwise, employed by the women in our family as they struggled with many of the same issues we face today. We depend on these to tell us about being a woman: our role in society, our relationships, our sexuality. Our family legends influence the formation of female traditions and expectations of how women within this family should act and define what the future may hold for us.

Melissa heard from her earliest years about the beauty of her family's women and how they used it to their advantage. Her great-grandmother Sarah used her beauty to circumvent oppressive family rules. Sarah's very religious Jewish family became enraged when she expressed her desire to model hats. Undaunted, Sarah argued that the money she earned could be used to put her older brother through medical school. This won her argument, and Sarah became the first woman in the family to work outside the home.

Sarah's action created a tradition that encouraged women in her family to participate in more public forums. As a result, Sarah's niece went to college to earn a teaching degree. With the self-confidence that her beauty instilled in her, she won honors on the debate team.

She went on to teach and became a noted academician. With this as a tradition, it is no wonder that Melissa, who has already won Miss Junior Miss from her state, is now considering an acting career.

Stories may also serve to define the relationships a woman will have with her husband, her children, and other family members. What does it mean to be a good wife? A good daughter? A good mother? These roles vary from family to family. Some families are matriarchies, where women dominate their quiet husbands. In other families, the women serve their husbands in long-suffering silence. In some families, the women are considered the smart and savvy ones; in others, women are foolish and frail.

A friend told me a favorite family tale of hers. "One story I heard throughout my life was about my great-great-aunt Verity. She lived in England and had the misfortune to be married to an alcoholic seaman. My uncle would sign on to a ship, take the money, get drunk, and miss the sailing date. Each time he did, Verity, who worked as a cook for a middle-class family, would become enraged. She'd yell at him, sometimes beat him, and always threaten to throw him out.

"Well, one time he signed on to a ship and swore on the family Bible that he would make it this time, that nothing could keep him from his obligation. But the usual happened. He went out to celebrate, got drunk, and fell asleep on a street corner. He was afraid to go home to his wife, so he stayed away. Only when he read of the disastrous sinking of the *Titanic,* the ship he was scheduled to sail on, did he dare to venture home. Aunt Verity, who had thought him dead, was so happy to see him that she never yelled at him again.

"The assumption behind this story was that Aunt Verity saw the error of her ways and mended them," my friend said. "In my family this tale has always been taken as saying, Never push your man; you could lose him. In the back of my mind I've always heard the warning, No husband will be perfect; settle for one that's 'good enough.'

"Although all the women in my family learned this lesson, we dealt with it in different ways: my mother picked a man who was so stubborn, she seemed to have no influence on him; my grandmother treated my grandfather so tentatively, she seemed afraid that he would break. I, on the other hand, seem to be afraid to commit myself to a man, knowing I'll have to live with 'good enough.' "

Recognizing a story's implied message and its effect on us is the first step to understanding the value these stories have for us. It can free us to choose the legacy that fosters our resilience and set aside the lessons that detract from it. My friend, already in the process of addressing her fear of commitment in relationships, found this favorite story indicative of the beliefs with which she had been raised. Knowing their source, she could more easily refute them.

Stories that Transform

Whether nurturing or restricting, we share these traditions with other women in our families. We can see them as an important influence on our mothers and aunts, as well as ourselves. As we come to understand their messages, these stories become a way of understanding our mother and the pressures under which she lived, the decisions she made, and the circumstances she faced as she raised us.

These new understandings can aid in our personal development, even alter our relationships. They enable us to see our present circumstances within a wider context and to look past our present relationship with our relatives. In stories about our mother as a child or young woman, the experiences that molded her, her relationships in her own family and with her own mother, we may see her, perhaps for the first time, not as the most powerful woman in our life, but as a person like us, who also had to discover her way.

Janice told me, "My mother was always so strong, so perfect, it seemed. She made everything look so easy. No wonder the idea of growing up was scary to me. How could I ever learn to be the strong and confident woman my mother was? She never seemed to have doubts or hesitations. I felt I was growing up in her shadow, filled with self-doubt.

"Then, the summer I was getting ready to go away to college, my mother told me how terrified she had been at college. How difficult it was for her to be away from home. It was so wonderful to hear this side of her, I made her tell me everything about her college days. It was as if a door had opened. I learned, really learned, that everyone has doubts and fears about new situations. And it brought me closer to my mother. Suddenly she was more than my mother, she became a friend, an equal. It was a turning point in our relationship."

Many women, like Janice, find it difficult to compare themselves with their mother, especially if they differ in such personal attributes as temperament, skills, and preferences. This contrast may make us doubt our decisions and ability to fulfill expectations of us as women. In such cases, it may be especially important for us to learn about other women in our families. Such a view can allow us to see beyond our mother's example to other role models within the family.

Throughout her life, Audrey identified strongly with her father's temperament and love of literature but felt awkward and out of place with her mother and sisters.

"I grew up feeling like the ugly duckling, since my sisters inherited my mother's good looks and flair for dressing," said Audrey. "I had no talent or interest in that. As a lifelong bookworm, I am casual, even careless, about my looks. As I grew older, more and more of my relatives began to compare me to my father's mother, a published children's author. When I was sixteen, my father gave me the diary my grandmother had kept at that age. Suddenly, I felt connected in an important way to the past and other parts of my family I hadn't known of before. I saw that there are many choices for women in my family, not only my mother's and sisters' choices, but also my grandmother's way—and my way."

The riches contained in these traditions are not limited to knowledge of how to conduct ourselves within our family or how to establish a better relationship with our mother. As the role of women in our society continues to be redefined, our family legacy often holds the wisdom of how our ancestors managed change and may hold the key for what will work for us. As we look within for solutions to the problems and difficulties in our lives, again our family history may contain clues to point us in the right direction.

"I was raised in an agnostic household," said Marsha, a woman of balanced resilience. "Religion was just not part of what we learned, although both sides of my family had been deeply religious until my parents' generation. My great-aunt Mary had been a nun in a contemplative order. As a girl, I was always intrigued by the life she must have led and her choice to live secluded from the world, to give up marriage and children. I imagined how deep her faith must have been. I often imagined her faith as tested as the faith of the holy saints.

"Last year when my daughter died, I broke down completely. Everything seemed utterly futile. I envied all the people I knew who had a religious practice, a way of worship, a faith in the goodness of the universe. I began to think of my great-aunt in a different way. I remembered the stories I'd made up about her great faith and began to think seriously about going back to the Church. Eventually I did, much to my family's amazement. It was a big part of the answer I needed."

Dark Legacies

The influence family stories have on our understanding of the world can be negative as well as positive. Far from strengthening or encouraging our resilience, they may serve to create shame or foster a sense of powerlessness. They represent the dark side of our legacy and speak of the unacceptable aspects of our family or its members. They may be admonishments about bad or wrong behavior, or they may involve an important decision that turned out badly. They may be used to justify extreme cautiousness or to keep us to tried and true behaviors. "Don't be different," they may tell us, "or look what will happen!" Other dark legacies may serve to put the blame for our circumstances outside our control and give away our power.

April remembered the stories of her grandmother, who at the height of the Great Depression, turned down a proposal from a wealthy man she did not love to marry her sweetheart, a penniless man unable to support her and their family.

April said, "Every time things weren't going well financially, my family would drag out this story. Every time my father was laid off or money was especially short, my mother would repeat again and again how the family could have been a lot better off—if only grandmother had swallowed her pride and done what was smart. I guess my folks were afraid to look forward; it seemed easier to look back on what might have been. They would imagine what they could have done with the money grandmother did not marry into. And they would get angry at her for being the one person they could point to who had access to money but didn't choose it.

"I guess it's no wonder my brother Sean always talks about winning the lottery; he travels around to four states sometimes just to buy tickets. And it seems my sister's always waiting for some sweepstakes celebrity to come to the door. She and her husband would rather do that than train for better jobs or move to a place they could find better-paying work."

Stories such as this one help to maintain the family's belief that money is something difficult to obtain. Real wealth, it says, is only possible through personal connections or wild luck. It narrows the family's vision of how they might become self-sufficient and devalues their ability to provide for their needs.

In this way a family's legacy can serve to clip the wings of its members and keep them from imagining a different life. While the motive of telling such stories may be to protect us from following these disastrous ways, the result may be to trap us by not showing an alternative. Family stories may express fear of failure, helplessness, hatred, or shame. They may instill fear and sense of the futility. They take away our resilience, deny our inherent strengths, and put responsibility for events outside of our control.

Accepting or Rejecting Our Stories

In some cases, dark legacies may serve as a form of self-fulfilling prophecy. Cilla, whose overwhelmed resilience has kept her trapped in self-defeating cycles, said, half ironically, half in earnest, "Miller women are never lucky with men; we always fall for the losers. This was the belief I was raised with, and I am a walking testimony to this. At forty I've been married four times. I'm just beginning to figure out that I've been proving my mother, aunt, and grandmother right by making the same mistakes that they did. Believe it or not, it is scary to think about being happily married. I just wouldn't fit into my family."

For Cilla, a happy marriage would leave her isolated, cut off from the camaraderie that exists between the women as they complain to one another about their husbands and their treatment by men. It may be that her family's beliefs have contributed to the failure of her marriages because of such attention to negative detail.

"Now at least I can complain with the best of them," she says, "I guess we all have this common identity. We are all the victims of men. But imagine if I were happy. I'd have no one to talk to!"

Until Cilla realizes that she can reject this identity and make other choices, she may continue to find only the destructive relationships promised by her family.

We may not want to disprove a family myth for fear of being disloyal. It takes resilience to find our own path. Dawn, a woman of stellar resilience, recalls her mother's particularly negative reaction to Dawn's plan to open her own gift shop. Her mother said, "You know, we don't have what it takes to succeed in business. Remember your uncle Bill. You're just like him. He always thought he could do more than he could, and look where it landed him. Dependent on grandmother. I don't want you doing this to me."

Later Dawn realized how farfetched her mother's objection had been. Dawn said, "Uncle Bill, bless him, knew nothing about the food business, let alone restaurant management, when he opened his diner. And he borrowed all the money to finance the venture. No wonder he failed. Despite my mother's insistence, I'm not at all like Bill. I've worked as a gift store manager for fifteen years, and a store clerk before that. I've got most of the money I'm going to need for the first year already in my savings account.

"My mother's reaction was so telling: 'I'm only trying to protect you from our family failing. You know none of us has any business sense.' It explained a lot to me about the choices my mother has made in her life and the caution my father always exercised. I hadn't realized how strongly Mom felt about her older brother's failures or how she blamed him for their mother's early death."

Dawn had the courage not to take her mother's admonitions to heart and the insight to see how much her family's lifestyles were tied together. Once she saw these family traits, she began to look further at the messages she had been given. It began an important line of inquiry for Dawn.

Unfortunately, it is usually difficult to overcome long-learned family lessons, and it may require some time and effort before we learn enough about our resilience to create new legacies. Yet when we recognize these dark legacies for what they are, we can confront them, looking deeper into their messages and their implications for ourselves. We can examine them rationally and accept or reject their lessons on the basis of who we are, and we can begin to entertain new views of the world.

Personal Meanings

In some stories we find a special resonance that means more to us than to others. Just as we have a favorite fairy tale or childhood story, we may find ourselves drawn to particular family stories and not others. We may be attracted to stories that lend us wings and take us to where we would like to go, or to stories that clarify our understanding of the people we care about, or to stories that reflect where we are now in our lives. Stories about our father's problems in school, for example, may appeal to us greatly as a child, as stories of grandmother's elopement may appeal to us in adolescence.

These favorite stories speak to us in a special, intuitive way. They feed our deepest images, our most personal conceptions. Our understanding of these stories and their meaning for us will depend on our unique personality. The same story will affect different people in different ways or will take on different meanings over time. So even as we hear the same stories as our siblings or parents, each of us hears a slightly different tale, according to our temperament, experiences, and emerging understanding of ourselves.

Gloria and her sister Melanie loved to hear stories about their grandmother, who endured her husband's infidelity, but never lost her spirit and never took her heartbreak out on her children. Gloria felt herself to be following carefully in her mother's footsteps and so identified with her mother and her mother's mother. Melanie, however, had a much quieter temperament than her sister and felt like an outsider in the family. She identified with her grandfather's mistress, a young servant who could never hope to be accepted into the family's Viennese aristocratic lifestyle.

As legacies born of personal insights and understanding, there is no right version of a story. A story and its values change as we change and mirror our altered perspectives.

How Stories Change

Stories are as much a reflection of the teller as they are about the subject. What story we choose to tell and what aspects of it we choose to emphasize have a great deal to do with the issues we are currently struggling with, as well as our beliefs.

As Thelma was growing up, her mother, May, used to tell her what a difficult child she was, stubborn, ill-tempered, unkempt. May would remind her daughter frequently that her labor was long and painful and that Thelma was the reason she had given up her promising career.

When Thelma herself became a mother, May continued to tell stories about her, but the stories were markedly different. No longer burdened by caring for a child, May began instead to speak about her daughter's fierce independence rather than the difficulty of caring for her. When her granddaughter would cry, May would tell her how strong Thelma had been and how she'd never cried, even when she received six stitches.

As we resolve conflicts, as May was able to with the birth of her granddaughter, we can move to a different vantage point that allows us to remember the past differently. May now had a grandchild to nurture without the responsibility of being the primary caretaker. This allowed her to remember her daughter in a new way that involved less of her own fear of being a mother. Her stories became more about her daughter and less about the anxieties her daughter produced in her. The same process often takes place when family members die and their shortcomings lose importance beside their more admirable qualities.

How Meanings Change

Even the same stories can take on different meanings for us at different times of our lives. Given our growth, our development, we often gain a perspective that can challenge prevailing notions within our family's oral history. Ella said, "When I was fifteen, my mother told me her brother was so smart when he was my age that he would write term papers for his college friends. He would ask them what grade they wanted and write a composition to order. When I first heard this, I took it as proof of my uncle's great intellect and scholastic aptitude.

"As an adult looking back, however, I see it in another way. It seems now just one more sign of how seldom my uncle applied his considerable talents on his own behalf, turning them instead into something to give away, a parlor trick for show," Ella said.

"Now I see him as someone who missed out on what he could have been. I guess you could say that both interpretations are valid. My mother still clings to the belief of her brother's brilliance, while I see past this into the waste of his talents."

Finding Our Own Way

Discovering the personal meanings in family stories is necessary if we are to move past our family's interpretations of events and find our own definitions. As we develop resilience and independence from others' ways, we will find our stories change, too. We can aid this natural evolution through consciously choosing the stories we tell and the meanings we ascribe to them. Through these stories, we may define for others what we see as the important images of our family. Through retelling our favorite stories, we can keep alive the memory of an important person or time in our lives. We can begin to select the legacy we choose to live by and pass on to our children.

"My mother-in-law died before Camilla was born," said Lori. "She and I were very close, and it was a great sorrow for me that she never lived to see her granddaughter. She was a doctor, a heart surgeon, at a time when that was much less common than now. So I take down the family photo albums from time to time, and we look at the pictures and talk about the people. Camilla is curious about her grandmother. I tell her all the stories I can remember. She was a good model for my daughter."

In the case of unpleasant stories, we can use our resilience to understand what it is we dislike about them. What is it they say and how can we revise them?

Martha told me, "When it comes to family histories, I had a hard time accepting mine. We were weaned on tales of my great-grandfather selling healing potions at the county fair in the late 1800s, potions he'd cook up with whatever was around. Then there were the tales of my uncle being so good at selling previously wrecked used cars to unsuspecting buyers. Eventually he was sent to jail for tax evasion.

"When I was a little girl, I was so ashamed to think that my relatives were a pack of common criminals and charlatans. I told everyone my uncle was dead or that my mother was an only child."

As Martha grew up and had more experience in the world, her attitude about her relatives changed. She began to see other qualities about her relatives, such as their ability to live by their wits. "I still abhor their lawlessness and willingness to victimize others," said Martha, "but I realize also that they were independent people, not afraid of taking risks for that they want. They liked living life on the edge. This appeals to me.

"So I'm finding my own way of being true to my values. I need to, as a lesbian expecting my first baby. It's a risk, but my life-partner and I are thrilled. And so is my family. Now that I've made peace with myself and with being unconventional, it's easier to see my connection to my heritage."

Part of our development comes from a very natural desire to stand outside of our family system for a while so that we can see ourselves and our family more clearly. Finding our own way means using what works for us. Whether we accept or reject our family's stories and the lessons they convey, they can still play an important role. After all, rejecting a negative legacy may nevertheless point us in the right direction. If our own solution is prompted by our family's lack of one, then in a funny way we still have them to thank for our inspiration.

Resilience can help us look beyond what our family offers us to what we need in our lives. If we must, we can rewrite our legacy to champion new heroes and offer new understandings of old events. We can choose to adopt our family's beliefs as our own, or begin to take from them what we need for our roots or our wings. We are free to put to rest what we cannot or do not want to use.

My Family's Legacy

Think for a moment of a favorite family story. Pick one that had special meaning for you, and write it down.

Now look at your story and consider the following questions. Encourage your resilient voice to provide answers. You can write down your responses if you wish for later reference.

- What is it that you liked so much about the story?
- How did you understand this story as a child, and what was it teaching you?
- How do you understand this story now? Has your understanding of its message changed with time?
- If this story changed in meaning for you, what does the change tell you about your own growth?
- Is its lesson still valid in your life today? Do you still use this story? Do you tell it to your children, your friends?
- How does it make you feel to have this story part of your personal history?
- What coping styles does it convey? Are they relevant to you today?

CHAPTER 6

Adolescence, Women, and Society

woman's identity is shaped not only by her family and personal experiences, but also by the values and female traditions that extend beyond her family. As she matures and begins to move away from her family and their influences, a young woman comes up against the lessons and values of the larger society and culture in which she lives. These, too, help to shape her identity and her resilience.

Society's influence is a subtle blend of repetitive images, clear sanctions, and promised rewards for compliance. We find society's messages in the entertainment media, in advertising, in art and literature, at school, in religious and social institutions, in peer groups, and in the larger community. These messages are unrelenting, enfolding a young woman every moment of every day. They tell her how she should look, how she should behave, what is expected of her.

Making sense of these messages is difficult because so many of the messages and images are contradictory. Women may be seen as "asking for trouble" if they dress stylishly, but as peculiar if they do not. A woman is selfish if she tries to "have it all"—raising children, holding a job, and needing child care—but also if she does not have children or delays starting a family while she establishes a career. Despite the many cultural sanctions against abortion, women who keep their children and need public assistance are looked down on by many and often regarded as freeloaders.

This list of contradictions could be much longer. Ultimately, the issue is less how society depicts us than how we interpret these messages for ourselves. Do we use these pressures to allow ourselves to be boxed and labeled, frustrated and powerless? Or do we use the very nature of these conflicting messages as permission to choose an identity consistent with our own beliefs? The answers to these questions depend upon our ability to develop and heed our resilient voice.

The Adolescent Pressure Cooker

Adolescence is the critical period in a woman's life when she actively begins to seek her own identity and determine her own lifestyle. It is a time she naturally desires more independence from her family and begins to enter more completely into the world beyond her parents' immediate control. In traditional societies, adolescence is a time of initiation into the ways of adulthood and the role a woman will assume. Many women benefit from deep and lasting friendships begun at this time, particularly with teachers, counselors, or other older women who can act as mentors for their developing resilience.

Today, most young women receive far less guidance than in the past. They are left instead to make their own way through the barrage of societal messages, the seemingly endless array of choices and possibilities. For a number of reasons, this can be a treacherous time for women, especially for those who have not yet developed an inner sense of self or not yet begun to draw on their resilience.

Much has been written concerning the difference in social and emotional development between boys and girls, beginning in earliest childhood. Typically boys are represented as more concerned with winning and girls with sharing, cooperating, and protecting of others' feelings. This theory has been used to explain why in adulthood men are more concerned with competition and women with relationships. Yet there is more to it than these basic orientations, according to Carol Gilligan, a clinical psychologist and researcher.

Throughout childhood, notes Gilligan, girls are socially and physically more mature than boys at the same age. With adolescence, however, a curious thing happens. In her research on the subject, Gilligan found "morally articulate pre-adolescents" transformed into hesitant, apologetic young women who began each statement of opinion with a denial of its importance. Why? she asked.

Gilligan's findings indicate that adolescent girls learn to adjust their personalities to conform to cultural norms. In their sensitivity to others, girls soon discover that exposing their own point of view in many situations is not acceptable for girls and threatens their social acceptability. This becomes generalized to an understanding that self-assertion is undesirable and even dangerous. As a result, girls shut down their resilient voice and developing sense of self in an effort to adapt to what they believe society expects from them.

In this way, girls learn to censor what they are thinking and begin to hide what they know even from themselves. They actively move from independence toward dependence in order to be judged acceptable. In their dependent role, girls begin to assume responsibility for caring for others. These messages combine to suggest that to care for others women must sacrifice self, which often causes them to neglect their own care.

The result is an uneven development of their resilience that continues into adulthood. This can contribute to paradoxical, undeveloped, and self-contained patterns of resilience, as these girls may not develop the ability to make choices based on their own needs. They may hide their emerging identity and capacity for self-direction, or focus intensely on conforming.

Chloe was a gifted math student all through junior high, but in high school her academic performance fell off, most noticeably her math. When her parents became concerned, she explained that she felt bad for the kids who were not as smart. She was tired of being held up as the standard that others should emulate. It was easier, she found, to do less well in school than to have her friends feel bad for not being as smart. Chloe took care of her friends by doing less well in school.

Ironically, the transformation Gilligan documents occurs at the time when girls most need to challenge the authority and values of their parents. The result for some young women is that they lose touch with their roots and focus only on their wings. This may constitute a serious trap for girls who have particular reason to reject their family, as in the case of incest or other abuse. They become sponges for what society has to offer, but do so at the expense of developing an inner foundation that allows them to balance these opposing forces. One classic example of this is Marilyn Monroe. She had very little rooted-ness, but captured the world's attention with her wings. She kept reaching out to be what others wanted her to be, but had very little inner sense of self. Many believe this sense of emptiness led to her early death.

Reinforcing Resilience

The answer to this situation is to encourage each young woman to learn to listen to herself and develop an inner dialogue with her resilient voice. This can be accomplished through journal writing, poetry, and other forms of self-expression.

Other positive feedback can be the communication of thoughts and feelings with peers, perhaps through groups that can help girls explore the challenges they confront in adolescence. School projects that encourage cooperation, such as group writing or art projects, give girls a positive learning environment. Many young women find it more motivating to receive a group grade rather than an individual grade. It is important, too, that teachers call on girls in class, ask their opinions, and show them that their opinions count.

The desire for acceptability and positive social interaction is not in conflict with the development of a strong sense of self. In fact, when they are combined, they give a young woman a formidable power.

Your Developing Self

Allow your resilient voice to answer the following questions as you believe you would have answered at age eleven and at age fifteen and then as you would answer them now.

- Do you think it's good to have your own opinions?
- Do you feel good about your opinions?

- What issues do you have strong feelings about?
- What is the object of your concern?
- How do you share your opinions?
- Can you remember a time you fought for your opinion?
- How does it feel to have strong opinions?
- Whom do you talk to about your opinions?
- What is their reaction to you?
- Whose opinions do you most respect: your own, your parents', others' [name]?
- Whose counsel do you heed most often: your own, your parents', others' [name]?
- Is that right for you? Is it in your best interest?

- What are the consequences for your self-esteem?

Look over what you have written. Has their been a shift in your focus between age eleven, age fifteen, and the present? Why?

Women in the Media

In a media-oriented society we all experience pressure to define ourselves in the context of our lifestyle. Values are attached to the acquisition of everything from stockings to hair dye, each product promising to grant us specialness in some way, playing upon our desire to be accepted and liked. We are bombarded with messages about such transitory sources of identity such as style—having dresses of the right length, driving the right car, eating the right food, and being seen at the right restaurant. Self-care is no longer the practice of tried and true methods, but may appear attainable in a series of quick pain-relief products, each stronger and faster than the next.

Our entertainment choices also present models by which we may shape our identity. On the radio, songs assure us that eternal love and devotion are possible. Models and sports stars demonstrate how we should look. Each image holds out the elusive promise of less pain and greater connectedness. TV shows point out what we lack by exposing us to all there is. Even the most serious problems—the dissolution of a family, drug addiction, or trauma such as rape—can all be resolved in thirty or sixty minutes, less time for commercial interruption.

These images serve as guidelines for how to live and lead us to feel that we need to be efficient, independent, successful, ever youthful, healthy, and energetic. These messages tell us that as workers we should be positive, unemotional, and proficient. As mothers we should be able to juggle career and family, and keep up our home and appearance. As lovers we are led to expect that each embrace will be passionate, each sexual encounter will lead to fulfillment, and that relationships are lifelong and faithful.

The challenge of living in a media driven society is learning how to use the media to our advantage, rather than being overly influenced and abused by it. It takes clear determination to wrest the best from these messages to allow them to be the inspiration for our wings, rather than to entrap us.

Lydia came from a working-class family and planned to find a secretarial position when she graduated. "But when I saw the movie *Working Girl,* I realized that there was more," said Lydia. "I didn't have to be limited by my background. If Melanie Griffith's character could learn to talk differently, walk differently, act differently, dress differently, then I could, too. I knew I couldn't get there all at once, but seeing her do it gave me the determination to achieve it."

Lydia decided to take accounting courses at a community college. "I wanted to learn more about business and eventually work at the stock market," she said. At college she met another ambitious young woman and together they took an apartment in downtown Manhattan.

"Today I work for a brokerage house, learning about trading stocks and bonds," said Lydia. "I'm still in school. I feel good about the changes I've made. Recently a new professor at college asked me where I was from. When I said Staten Island, she asked where my accent was. I was thrilled. I feel I'm on my way."

Unfortunately, the effects of the media can be less favorable, especially for the adolescent just building her identity. Tabitha came to see me for depression. In our discussions she told me she had stopped reading a popular girls magazine. When I asked why, she said that it depressed her to see all these smiling models with perfect hair and teeth and to read stories about the heroines doing well in school.

"It's just too phony," said Tabitha. "School is hard work. I can't spend all my time, let alone my college money, worrying about how good I look. I've got to get real. To tell you the truth, I'm scared to death I don't have what it takes to make it. The magazines make you think that anything less than perfection just isn't enough."

Although Lydia and Tabitha may appear to be at opposite points in their developing identities, they share much in common. They both recognize the fact that media images are idealized and not representative of everyday reality for most girls their age. Both have a strong sense of who they are and the desire to concentrate on achieving their self-determined goals.

While Tabitha felt temporarily overwhelmed, she knew where she stood. Later she developed an interest in the life of Emily Dickinson, a poet who also struggled with her own feelings of self-worth.

Other girls are not as fortunate as Tabitha or Lydia, whose resilience is developing in healthy, balanced ways. Adolescents who are in the process of forming undeveloped or overwhelmed resilience, for example, are more likely to be driven by what they see around them. Already fearing that they are different, they are more susceptible to any perceived rejection. They may hope to find inner meaning and security in learning to conform to constantly changing external criteria. I have known young girls who believe very seriously that their self-worth is determined by having every color of the latest designer jeans. Not having them is cause for feelings of sincere self-deprecation and anxiety.

Women who define their self-worth by such external possessions and standards are searching for an anchor that can't be found in this way. Instead they need to identify the source of the pressure they feel and to listen to their own inner dialogue. If they are lucky, they can find role models and mentors to reinforce the development of their resilience and show them the value of their inner worth.

Responsibility for Our Bodies

I remember one summer day in New York City when I was in my mid-twenties. I was dressed comfortably in shorts and a T-shirt, walking in my neighborhood. I was feeling good. Then I passed a construction site and the wolf calls started. I was propositioned, looked at lasciviously. I became frightened. I no longer felt good about myself, I felt guilty that I had caused this reaction. I felt responsible for it. I also felt shaken and incredibly vulnerable.

Many of us have had these moments when we blamed ourselves for someone else's physical feelings for us, for someone else's need to shame us in order to gain more power, prominence, sexual potency. For the adolescent this represents a potentially confusing choice. As she is responded to sexually, she needs to determine how she will respond. The media promulgate an image that encourages her to be desirable, but only she can determine for herself how to react.

Some teens react to their new desirability by acting out promiscuously. They attempt to please, and in their desire for independence, they may reject the values of their family. They also may be confused by their new independence and lack of experience. In their confusion, they may feel trapped in their new choices.

It is unfortunate but true that sometimes we learn best through our most painful choices. Adolescence often is a time of painful choices, but it is precisely the pain in these choices that makes this a crucial time for the growth of resilience.

It may seem strange to view attractiveness as a liability, yet it is often very difficult for a woman to be both competent and attractive, especially for teens. Many learn to hide their brightness, skills, or beauty as a way of fitting into the world of work or school. Some women suppress all aspects of their brightness and remain with undeveloped resilience or practice a paradoxical approach to their strengths: they may save their brightness for work and give in to their spouse at home, or maintain their beauty at home and be overly careful and awkward at work.

One student teacher I counseled had a problem at work of being too beautiful. With long, flowing blonde hair and a winning smile,

Moira attracted the love of the fourth graders she taught and the jealousy of the other teachers.

"One teacher in particular always leaves me feeling humiliated after I speak with her," said Moira. "She never criticizes me directly—it's always some procedure that she hones in on. Even though she is not overtly attacking me, I feel that I need to protect myself. Some days I feel like crawling into the corner and hiding. I'm afraid it's affecting my ability to do my work."

When I asked Moira to think about what was going on, she paused and said, "Somehow, although nothing has been said, I know it has more to do with the fact that she finds it difficult to work with me than with anything I've done."

When she stopped to reflect and listen to what her resilient voice could tell her about the situation, Moira realized the other teacher had the problem, not she. When we spoke about it in this way, Moira felt freed. She said, "I felt that I could come out of hiding and be more of myself. I still find myself saying the same placating things to her, but I feel clearer now that I've realized that she just is uncomfortable around me."

Many women never resolve this confusion over how others respond to them. Women who aspire to power may choose to hide their beauty and deemphasize their sexuality rather than call attention to this part of themselves. They adopt a different demeanor at work, neutral dress, little makeup, no perfume. They do this because it is safer to be less sexual, less of a threat, and look more of the part that they wish to play. An imbalance occurs, however, when the need to fit in or obtain others' approval becomes so great that they seek to hide or alter who they are in an effort to conform. Doing so makes it difficult for women to feel acceptable for all of who they are rather than specific roles they assume.

"I wouldn't dare dress at work the way I dress at home or with friends," Gail explained. "None of the women in my office would wear anything but business suits and simple dresses. I sometimes feel like an imposter when I'm sitting in a staff meeting, but it's part of the game. My closet is like my life—divided into work on the one side and play on the other, with a big space in between."

Gail was channeling so much of her energy at work into trying to fit in, to answer the expectations of the hospital administrators where she worked. I could hear the strain in her voice every time she talked about her work. It was indicative of Gail's style of paradoxical resilience.

Other women feel their beauty is an integral part of who they are; they enjoy the benefits of developing this side of themselves. Women of balanced resilience seem to integrate this aspect into their personalities more easily.

"I'm attractive," said Rica, "and I think that's why people listen to me. I know it gives me an advantage over other people. I feel just as comfortable highlighting my physical attributes as my intellectual and creative attributes. People enjoy having me around."

On Our Own

The end of adolescence represents a crucial time for the development of our resilience, as we prepare to begin life on our own. We must define the degree of risk and challenge we are willing to accept and the extent to which we can integrate our inherent strengths into our emerging self-concept. Here we encounter the forces that will mold our adult identity and begin to develop our characteristic responses to these stressors and our unique style of resilience. As a girl matures, these forces and responses may become fixed patterns that are carried into adulthood until attempts at change and growth are made.

Michelle, twenty-one, is about to graduate from college and is terrified at the prospect. "I have always been taken care of," she said. "I don't know how to get a job, find an apartment, or even balance a checkbook. My parents have always done everything for me. I don't know if I'm ready to be on my own. At the same time, I've always dreamed of having my own place, a little studio apartment. I want to take art lessons and maybe some dance. I'd like to try that, even if it's scary to think of it."

Michelle, with undeveloped resilience, has been so dependent upon her parents that she has not developed a sense of confidence in her own abilities. It would not be unusual for such a young woman to marry in order to have someone continue to take care of her. She might take refuge in being a wife and mother, responding to the requirements of these two well-prescribed roles, and never have to face her own identity and deeper self. If she did, it would be a loss, for she would lose the chance to gain more out of life by learning these facts about herself.

Fortunately, Michelle has at least a small vision of what she could have on her own to balance against her desire for protection. That is a hopeful sign, for it signals that her resilient self is struggling to be heard.

Laurie is more balanced in her resilience. She, too, struggles with the part of herself that wants to be protected, but she has formed her own plan to move out into the world. After graduation from high school, Laurie found a job in a clothing store in a nearby city. She loves men's fashion, much to her parents' chagrin. Laurie continues to live at home, saving her money so that she can attend the Fashion Institute of Technology in New York City. This also displeases her parents, but Laurie is clear on her goal, and this allows her to resist their pressure. By not taking on too much too soon, Laurie is able to face these new challenges with stamina and resolve. She will gain experience and confidence as she continues to master this first important step toward independence.

Marguerite is at a crossroads. Academically gifted, she is well on her way to developing stellar resilience if she can learn to claim her talents, or paradoxical resilience if she doesn't. Even though she graduated with honors from high school and won a full scholarship to the University of Michigan, Marguerite feels she has achieved this all by luck. She does not see her accomplishments as coming from her own abilities and so is not sure how to replicate them. This causes her great anxiety.

The daughter of an addict, Marguerite grew up in a series of foster homes, the only family life she ever knew. Each time it seemed she had settled in, her mother would show up and take her away again. Marguerite has come to feel that her life is governed by forces beyond her influence. If she is able to find her place at college among friends, for example, or become involved in her studies, she may be able to apply herself productively to her education. If so, she may well break through into stellar resilience by claiming her accomplishments. If not, she may continue to see her accomplishments as belonging to some capacity beyond her control and feel the need to partition off her competence and develop paradoxical resilience. In that case, she will have difficulty drawing on that competence to achieve goals in other important areas in her life, such as interpersonal relationships.

Helene has battled with her shame throughout her adolescence. She feels unworthy and has played this out by dating abusive boys. She is now pregnant and overwhelmed. She will not give up her child, clinging to the magical belief that by having this baby, she can right the wrongs done to her. She is so full of shame that she cannot admit her own neediness, her pain, or her fear. Yet Helene has an important asset—the desire for a better life for herself and her child. If she can focus on that goal, rather than her despair, she may yet discover the resources that will help her work productively toward it.

Amy's only identity has come from schoolwork. She knows she's smart, but that is all that she knows about herself. Her parents, who both have less than a high school education, have prided themselves on Amy's accomplishments. She has been in all the science honors classes in her high school, and she has even begun taking college-level math courses.

Amy doesn't date; she claims she doesn't have time. She's working on getting a full scholarship to Tulane University. She is edging toward self-contained resilience. When another area of her life seems difficult, Amy doubles her scholastic efforts. Amy needs someone, perhaps a mentor or classmate, to help her see that she is more than "an excellent student" and to encourage her to explore other facets of her personality, such as her sense of humor or her creativity.

The development and growth these women achieve in adolescence will determine much about the adult identity that will follow. Adolescence is a staging ground: a time in which childhood issues can be resolved and left behind, or linger to reemerge as issues in adulthood. As such, adolescence is a particularly important time in the development of a woman's resilience.

Changing Values

Building a healthy identity today is very different and in many respects more difficult than it was even a short time ago. In the past, a woman was defined by her association to family, community, and religious organizations. She was the caretaker, the bearer of children, the center of the family. In this there was power, and the certainty of knowing she was performing as expected. There was also great support.

In more traditional societies, a woman was more likely to feel satisfied in her role as mother and wife; this was in part due to her extended family. Another relative was always only a step away to take her child, allowing the mother a reprieve. The mother had an army of relatives ready to support her in her role, able to see the stress she labored under, and willing to lend expertise and encouragement. The child, too, had a fresh, trusted, and—most of all—connected series of adults to which she could turn to have her needs met.

In such societies obligations were not to oneself but to the group of which one was a part. In fact, the concept of self was not as strong; it did not need to be, for there was much support and certainty in group identity.

Many of these values characterized our own society until recently. Even a generation or two ago, our parents or grandparents were more concerned about their responsibilities to others—their sisters, brothers, parents, neighbors—than to themselves. As a member of a supportive family, each member enjoyed greater protection than we do now.

One example of this comes from the family of a friend of mine, Alice. As the youngest of four girls, Alice's mother was expected to stay home and care for her mother. This she did until she was twenty-eight, when one of her older sisters was established enough to have their mother come and live with her. During this time the sisters saved small amounts of money so that Alice's mother could continue her education. When the time came, Alice's mother left the rural community in which they all lived and went to secretarial school. Later she married and gave birth to my friend Alice.

"I grew up in a family of very strong aunts who continued to lend emotional support to one another and their children throughout their lives," said Alice. "In some ways it was like having more than one mother—whenever Mom was unavailable, one of my aunts was always there."

Extended families provided for many of the needs of the nuclear family, needs which now fall to an increasing number of single parents, usually women, who try to provide all that the extended family used to manage.

In any situation in life, there are trade-offs. While traditional societies provided support and security, they also stymied individual growth, particularly for women. So the shift away from traditional values also has its benefits. We are not as much dominated by class now as we once were. This allows someone like me, a woman born to a blue-collar family, to earn a Ph.D. But there is also a great deal we have lost, which we are still searching for.

We were as a society more cohesive, less mobile, more content. On an individual level we were less prone to the loneliness, quiet desperation, and the search for meaning in our life, than we are presently. When our connection to family, both immediate and extended, grew more tenuous, we became more isolated and more vulnerable. As a result we now face a new series of challenges concerning how to provide meaning in our lives. We question how to see ourselves, who we are, what we need. Having shed the identity markers found in our previous traditions and becoming increasingly resistant to the media's platitudes, we are now in need of new tools with which to understand and define ourselves. Perhaps our most important tool is our resilience.

CHAPTER 7

Issues in Adulthood

A favorite pastime in childhood is imagining our life as an adult. However, in recent years, it has become common to hear people in their twenties, thirties, or even forties, talking about what they will be when they "grow up." Although tongue in cheek, this comment is indicative of our ongoing uncertainty about ourselves and our ability to achieve all we should in life.

What does it mean to grow up, to be an adult? We may think of having the right to vote, owning and driving a car, holding down a job, or starting a family. These external measures signify a degree of functional maturity, but they do not necessarily address more essential aspects of adulthood.

Being an adult requires us to attain enough emotional and psychological independence to be our own person, assume responsibility for our needs, and live according to the values we set. Adulthood means that while we may not have all the answers, we have the courage to ask the necessary questions and take the next step. We don't wait for others' sanctions to claim our personal strengths and use them on our own behalf.

In adulthood we are presented with a changing array of challenges to be met and adjustments to be accomodated. This requires that each of us develop the flexibility and resources to weather these inevitabilities. No matter what coping styles we may have used in the past, we must continually create and realign strategies for the future. The emphasis, therefore, shifts from the style of resilience you may demontstrate now to how you can develop and enhance your resilience to address your future needs.

Our resilience is an invaluable ally in achieving this independence and shaping our adult identity. Through dialogues with our resilient voice, we can achieve a vantage point from which we can more clearly see who we are and what we need. This self-knowledge remains our guide as we move forward toward our goals, allowing us to weather transitions and problems, and to understand that through all of the changes in our lives, we have a rootedness that will see us through. Knowing who we are gives us a core of strength to meet the challenges and take the risks that will enable us to grow.

Separating Self from Family

Essential to the development of healthy independence is a woman's capacity to define herself as separate from her family. The normal tasks of adulthood usually move her in this direction: living on her own, holding a job, having a family of her own. Yet these alone are not enough to establish her as an independent person.

Carlyne and her mother had always had their differences. Carlyne said, "As the only daughter, I bore the brunt of my mother's hopes for a second chance in life. She never had the opportunity to study music, so I had to take violin lessons. She never went to her senior prom, so I should go to mine. The problem was, I didn't want either the violin lessons or the prom. Mom and I argued constantly throughout my teen years.

"Well, now I'm living two thousand miles away, thank goodness, and I'm on my own. My mom still checks up on me, but I just tell her what she wants to hear. She doesn't know my boyfriend's moved in with me. She doesn't think he's right for me, so I don't even tell her about him. I just hope she doesn't come to visit soon."

Carlyne is still in a power struggle with her mother, notwithstanding the geographical distance between them. She might as well be sixteen and living at home.

Like Carlyne, many people live their lives react to what others dictate, thereby according them great power over their lives. This is most common in young people whose resilience is undeveloped. As Carlyne matures and has more experience in making her own decisions, she will gain more confidence in her choices. She can stop reacting to her mother's opinions and find a lifestyle that matches her own values. She will see that true independence comes from being able to establish her life on her own terms, free from comparison to others, unencumbered by their values. It means being able to see others in such a way that they no longer have power over her.

This power can take many subtle forms. Alana, for example, with self-contained resilience, was adamant about her choice to set a different example for her children than her mother had for her.

"I love my mother, but frankly she wasn't much of a role model," Alana explained. "She was weak, ineffective in standing up for herself. She had great talent as a pianist, but never did anything with it. My father wouldn't even let her teach lessons. When I asked her why she gave up her career, she said a mother's place is with her children. I don't agree. Now that I'm expecting my first child, I've already decided I'm not going to give up my career. I want to show my child that a woman can be anything she wants."

Alana went back to work half-time when her daughter was three weeks old, and full-time when her daughter was two months. This time was very difficult for both mother and daughter, but Alana saw it through. Every time she thought about her decision, Alana reminded herself about what her mother hadn't been and what her own career would mean to her daughter. Alana never stopped to think about what was most important to herself at this time in her daughter's life. She wasn't thinking about her career in terms of her own goals or why her return to work was necessary just now. She was measuring her own choices against the disappointing choices of her mother. Alana had not yet learned that she could choose what was right for herself and did not need to fight her mother's battles.

Later in dialogues with her resilient voice, Alana realized that she had, in fact, followed her mother's pattern after all. Just as her mother had cut off her career to be a full-time mother to her family, so Alana was sacrificing her own enjoyment of this time in her daughter's life to fulfill her own expectation of what a mother could be. As she came to terms with this, Alana decided to make a change. Her first priority was to find a less demanding job closer to home.

"For the first time in years," Alana told me, "I feel I've found a balance I can live with. I think I've got the best of both worlds now."

The choices we make on all levels, from the foods we eat and the relationships we build, to where we live and how we spend our time, should reflect our values and personal needs. As we learn to listen more closely to our resilient voice on a day-to-day basis, we will see more clearly what belongs to us and what belongs to others.

Learning to Risk Feeling "Unpatriotic"

Achieving independence from our family is not a single step, but a process that unfolds over time. It is unique for every woman, depending upon her personality and circumstances.

Women begin this process of self-discovery, independence, and change at various times in their lives. Some confront this early on, especially in the case of a difficult childhood when a girl may find it necessary to distance herself from her family as early as the onset of adolescence. Other women, overprotected by their parents and then their spouses, may never undergo this process. For some, it may be precipitated by a major change, such as divorce, death, or major illness. The majority of women, however, experience this in early adulthood. For Claudia, it came as a gradual awakening.

"I always felt so thwarted whenever I tried to figure anything out," said Claudia. "I began to realize that if I was ever going to be independent, I would have to know who I was. This was a scary time, for I kept hearing a voice say that I was such a selfish girl.

"I'd look at myself in the mirror and didn't think I looked that selfish. I am twenty-eight, kind of cute and petite, but I don't fuss with myself. I rarely wear makeup, and all of my good clothes are for work. I put myself through school to get my M.B.A. In fact, all I seem to do is work; I rarely date. But strangely, I kept hearing the message that I'm selfish."

Claudia finally began to recognize whose voice it was. "It wasn't my resilient voice or my conscious mind," she said. "It was my mother. I had a running commentary in my head telling me that anything I did for myself was selfish: going to school or taking a job in another city. I began to listen more closely to my actual conversations with my mother, and sure enough, the message was there. I wondered how long had I been hearing this negative message without recognizing it. When I listened, it was clear as day: I was selfish if I moved away from my mother.

"It is interesting because my mother left home to go to college in another state, just like I did. And she had a career; I wasn't born until she was thirty-four. Yet somehow the expectation was there that I would always be around, needing her advice. I was selfish to be separate or want to be on my own."

But looking back, Claudia realized her mother seemed to be the original "Don't bother me, I gave at the office." She was never warm. Claudia can't remember her mother ever saying she loved her, and her mother rarely touched Claudia.

"I began to wonder what exactly my mother expected from me," said Claudia. "What did I owe her? I began to get angry at these unspoken expectations. This in turn brought up other incidents from the past that I hadn't thought of in years."

As a daughter begins to question her mother's values, traditions, and opinions, she may feel "unpatriotic," disloyal to what she has learned from her family, and to her mother in particular. She may question her family's interpretations of the many family legends and stories on which she was raised. She may see new meanings in what she once took for granted. It may seem as if she were seeing and hearing things for the first time. In beginning to question her family's rules and expectations, she may encounter her own dark side and, through it, entertain change.

Unconscious Beliefs

With the development of this new perspective, a woman begins to see unexplored alternatives. She learns to make changes more in keeping with her own wants and needs.

She may also experience a new awareness of her own beliefs and the conclusions that have governed her since girlhood and may be operating in her life as an adult. For example, a woman may suddenly become aware of a deep-seated belief that if she is competent, she will be abandoned—a fear many women of undeveloped resilience have. Or she may believe that if she is needy, she is being selfish—a fear common to women of overwhelmed and paradoxical resilience.

Although we have lived with these beliefs all our lives, they may remain so deeply buried that we are not even conscious of them. Claudia heard that she was selfish.

Claudia said, "I kept with it, trying to figure out what I wanted, who I was. Being away from home and recognizing my mother's voice was helpful. I became aware how much of my emotional energy was tied up in justifying my actions to her and second-guessing her responses to my decisions. In seeing this, I realized that there were new ways of living, new ways of creating traditions for myself and for my children to come. I could do things differently. I had the authority to change how I lived.

"I now encountered my mother and our relationship in a whole new light. Giving myself permission to have unpatriotic feelings, including anger toward my mother and other family members, actually allowed me to feel closer to my mother. She wasn't all-powerful; she was wrong about some things—about a lot of things, in fact. When I realized this, she became more approachable. Instead of being a monolith, she became a human being. I began to see the lonely and uncomfortable person that she was. My anger toward her began to exist side by side with my compassion for her and for myself.

"I experience her differently now with greater wisdom, less rancor. My understanding is tempered by my own experiences. My mother is not synonymous with who I am. That's becoming more clear to me all the time."

Making Peace with Our Parents

Developing the voice of her resilience helps a woman achieve independence by identifying what belongs to her. This allows a woman to make peace with her parents, frequently a crucial step in the development of her own identity and the recognition that as an adult, she can provide for her own needs, regardless of who her parents were or what they were and were not able to provide. A woman's ability to understand her inner capacity to nurture herself will relieve her parents, especially her mother, of the burden of having to meet all her needs. To understand her mother is also to understand herself, and her natural childlike wish for her mother to have been more than she ever humanly could have been. With this realization the daughter can use the voice of her resilience to assist and guide her in assuming responsibility for herself.

Claudia said, "My whole perspective changed when I realized that my mother offered me 100 percent of all she had. It may not have been much, for essentially my mother was an empty person. But she gave me what she could. My strengths are different from hers; this means I have different options. This realization helped me expand my horizons of what is possible.

"My mother was never close to her mother. She was the youngest of eleven children raised on a farm in Indiana. I remember her telling me that by the time she was born her mother was tired, worn out by so many kids and such a rugged life. My mother learned to be self-sufficient, self-absorbed, and totally willful. It was how she survived."

Recognizing the limitations of our mother allows us to see that we have adopted other mothers to nurture us, not only in our childhood but also in adulthood. Women in the workplace often look to an older, more experienced woman to learn the ropes of office politics or to learn additional skills in the laboratory or classroom.

Claudia found that she, too, had sought out other mothers. "Looking back," she said, "I see that even though I'm an only child, I always managed to find the sense of family I craved. I always had other people to take care of me. My father had two sisters, one of whom lived down the street from us. My aunt had a house full of kids but always seemed to have room for me, too.

"It was so much fun being there. Looking back, I see this was a pattern in my life, finding women, like my aunt or a favorite teacher, who took care of me in one way or another. Today it's my boss. She is tough, hard as nails, even difficult. But she has taken to me and is teaching me about the corporate world. I know how to get my needs

121

met from my interactions with others. I can give myself my own counsel. I owe that to my mother's influence.

"I have come to realize that in some ways my mother's coldness had its good side, too. We came to an understanding of how much she could give. As I realize who I am, I realize we have this in common. Now she needs to understand how much I have to give."

Identifying Your Unpatriotic Feelings

Take a moment to consider the following areas of daily life. Allowing your resilient voice to speak for you, consider what your own preferences and beliefs are in each.

- politics
- diet
- career
- child care
- housework
- sex
- dress
- friendship
- care of others
- care of self
- leisure time
- vacation

Now consider how your parents, especially your mother, think about each of these issues. Write this down. Look at the areas in which you differ from your parents, and check those issues that are the most difficult for you.

Identifying Our Personal Needs

As a therapist, I often see women who are struggling not with major life crises, but with a general sense of despair or hopelessness about their lives. Something is wrong, out of kilter; an important need is unmet. As a result, they are burned out and numbed. Most of the time, the essential problem is that they neglect their personal needs.

Our resilience can perform an important role in helping us to achieve a balance through the small choices we make every day: deciding how to spend our lunch hour, how to celebrate our mother's birthday, or how to nourish or challenge ourselves. Our resilient voice can steer us to more satisfying answers. Darla discovered this.

Darla said, "The first year we lived in Cincinnati, Alan and I used to go for a morning run together before work, even in winter. I loved that. I had no problem with my weight, and I felt good and energetic all day. When Alan changed jobs, however, he also changed his schedule. He didn't have time to go running, so I gave up running, too. I didn't like going by myself.

"After three months I had gained eight pounds and began to feel terrible about myself. I was so out of shape, even the thought of exercise wore me out. I tried various types of indoor exercise equipment and joined a gym, but all I could think of were those mornings running along the river. I knew it was that experience I needed. Some part of me wouldn't let me forget.

"So I began to think about how I could do that again. I started asking my co-workers if any of them enjoyed running. Sure enough, a friend of a friend was in a similar situation. I'm back running and I love it. I really missed that feeling."

I am frequently surprised at how little permission we give ourselves to make changes in our lives, to find alternatives to the inevitable roadblocks that come our way. Often all it takes is the ability to identify what we want, as Darla did, and find practical ways to balance it against the resources at our disposal.

Marsha was a mother, employed full time, who missed having time for writing poetry. The best time to write, she told me, was in the morning. She couldn't write then, though, because she needed to make breakfast for her sons, ages four and seven. I gave her an assignment: find a way to write half an hour every school morning and an hour every weekend morning.

The following week she told me, "I make their breakfasts and lunches the night before. I lay out their clothes and sign all the school notes while I watch the evening news. In the morning I get up fifteen minutes earlier than I used to, have half an hour to do my writing, and still have breakfast with the kids before we start our day. I've never been so organized in my life, but it's worth it. Every bit of it."

Giving ourselves permission to listen to our own needs is often difficult, especially for women of overwhelmed or self-contained resilience, who may never have felt entitled to name what they needed or to expend their resources on their own behalf. Some women have chosen not to acknowledge certain needs; others may not know how to formulate them. For women of paradoxical and self-contained resilience, their needs may be satisfied in certain areas of their lives, such as professional accomplishments or personal relationships, but not in other areas, a sign of their unbalanced resilience. Even women of stellar resilience may be so focused on other goals or certain areas of their lives that they overlook areas in which they remain needy.

It's important to take time to find out what you want. It may be something you used to do that you feel you no longer have time for or can't afford. It may be something you never even knew you wanted. Take time to listen to yourself, pay attention to your moods. Find out what really excites you, or what you dislike or dread about your life. Realize that by enriching your own life, you may well have more to contribute to the others around you. This process of discovery begins with listening to your resilient voice.

Standard of Weights and Measures

Some of our dissatisfaction with ourselves has less to do with our own values and expectations than external standards set for us by society in general. One of the most prevalent issues for American women is that of weight and beauty. Once again, we need to question our assumptions about these external pressures and determine what is right for us.

When it comes to physical appearance, women in western society are expected to fit within a very narrow framework. Nowhere is this more evident than in the area of weight. The fact that we are all different in height, bone structure, and build somehow eludes the societal norm that tells us that despite these differences we should all be the same dress size. Many women are willing to sacrifice, to literally starve themselves, in an effort to be more pleasing and have more worth.

I recall one women who consulted me about her bulimia. She was a sales representative in her early forties who had begun menopause and experienced some weight gain. As a result, she was purging herself. Her explanation almost broke my heart. Since she was in the public eye, she was afraid she would lose her job if she gained weight. "It would be the wrong image for my company," she said.

I know countless women who have struggled with feelings of inferiority all their lives because of their self-perceived lack of standard beauty or the unwanted attention they drew because of their attractiveness. With such an emphasis on physical beauty, positive or negative, it is no wonder that women frequently close off a part of themselves and separate their feelings about one part of themselves in order to cope with the rest of their lives.

When we exaggerate or overvalue one aspect of ourselves at the expense of another, we run the risk of losing our ability to perceive our full potential or to freely use all our strengths in our interactions in the world. We develop an unbalanced perspective of ourselves and our capabilities.

Ricky had always been heavy. Even when Ricky was a young girl, her mother tried everything she could think of to control her daughter's weight. As a teen, Ricky stuck to an extremely strict diet in order to lose enough weight to fit into the fashions her friends were wearing. She stayed at this weight until her first pregnancy, when she gained rapidly. After the birth of her child, the starvation regimen began, but she was unable to take the weight off.

"It became an obsession with me, I guess," said Ricky. "I refused to let Jon photograph me, even holding the baby. I didn't want to buy any new clothes, because they'd be in fat sizes. Instead, I held out the promise of a new wardrobe when I got down to 105 again. As a result, I had nothing to wear when we were invited to parties or special events. The worse I felt about myself and my weight, it seemed, the less I was able to do anything about it."

Ricky's anxiety about her weight fueled her self-doubt and other negative feelings about herself. This dark side began compromising her relationship with her husband, already strained by the birth of their son.

Ricky said, "It was difficult for me to acknowledge what was going on. How I was blackmailing myself, stuffing my fear and sense of hopelessness. I'd start these incredibly strict diets only to break them after a day or two. One day in the midst of my despair about not having anything acceptable to wear to a holiday function, I thought, I feel trapped, just trapped. Then I heard myself say, You're not trapped. You can do it; it just takes time. I can't tell you how good it felt to think, I can do it.

"Once I could look at the problem head on, I signed up for a weight management program. I bought myself a few attractive dresses in my present size and wore those until I'd lost enough weight to buy something new. I know I'll never be 105 again. It took everything I had to maintain my weight there. It was too big an effort.

"It's amazing to me now, but my weight is no longer a big issue in my life. I still attend weight-loss meetings and am conscious of eating only when I'm really hungry, but even that is no big deal any more. I feel attractive. I have energy for the more important things in my life, like my family and my job."

The overemphasis on standards of physical beauty lead many women to develop shameful feelings about themselves and their bodies. Like Ricky, they often suffer in isolation, unable to acknowledge the help they need to regain a balanced perspective of themselves. In confronting these feelings, women can allow their resilience to help them discover new options. It will aid them also in providing the self-love and resources they need to overcome the issues of their dark side.

Women and Work

Women have always worked. In early societies women's work put them at the center of community life. Women's responsibilities were well defined and in balance with their responsibility for bearing and raising children and other aspects of daily living.

Today women's work responsibilities are no longer as well defined. Most women work outside the home in jobs that isolate them from home and family for long hours each day. They frequently struggle with balancing home and work. At what stage should a mother return to the workplace, if at all? Is a mother's long absence from her children detrimental to their development? If we work the same hours in an office as our spouse, how much of the responsibility for housework and child care falls to us?

Ideas about all of these issues are still in flux. Without a norm to guide us, we may tend to doubt ourselves, no matter what choices we make. If we stay home to be a full-time mother, we may feel dissatisfied with this role or feel guilty that without our income, the family must do with less. If we work, we may miss the opportunity to spend enough time with our spouse and children.

If we are single, how much time should we devote to our career at the expense of our free time? How do we know when the stress of high achievement is too much or the compromise to our integrity too great?

Today, working is not a luxury for the millions of women who must support themselves and their families. Women in many fields find that they receive few promotions if they are perceived as likely to take time off for maternity leave (mommy tracking). Others find that positions above a certain level are unattainable for them—that they have encountered the glass ceiling.

We expect to be available for our family, provide for their needs, sit up with a sick child, and still keep up at the office.

In my experience, too few women realize the cost of this effort to their well-being, or the price to their self-image if they are unable to do it all to their own satisfaction. I counsel these women to spend some time looking at their daily and weekly schedules to realize the magnitude of what they expect from themselves. Then I ask them to ask themselves about their feelings. What is it they enjoy? What is it they dislike most about their lives, about their work life or home life?

As in other areas of thier daily lives, women may forget that here, too, they have options. The pressure to be a wage earner and parent may seem to set our lives in stone, leaving us few choices. In fact, we do have choices, if only in the way we think of our situation and ourselves. We need to recognize that there is no one right way to balance work and home. Yet no matter what our choice, when we take the time to evaluate our needs and the reasons for our choices, we can set aside self-doubt and take the credit for all we do.

Carol said, "I graduated valedictorian of my class at a top-rated liberal arts college. All my friends expected me to go on to gain my master's and doctorate. I know they were surprised when I not only didn't go to graduate school, but married a small-town minister instead of taking on a challenging career. Even my mother, who had to sacrifice to send me to college, made references to my wasting my education. Everyone asked, How could someone of such promise be satisfied as a minister's wife?

"I began to dread corresponding with my college friends or talking to them on the phone. 'Is that all you do?' 'Is that enough?' After a few years, I realized I felt ashamed to talk to them. I even caught myself asking, What is it that I do?"

Then Carol and her husband moved to a new parish. There were new faces to learn, new problems to confront, a new community to serve. "I began to observe myself and everything I did. I found myself organizing events, writing grants, working in the office, and chairing committees. Not a single skill I'd learned in twenty-five years went to waste," said Carol.

"After this time of soul-searching, I have a better perspective on myself and my choices in life. Many of my friends from college have tenured positions as professors at big-name universities; others are in government or the professions. They've built their lives around their academic interests or personal social commitment. I've built my life around the heart, around people and community. My life here allows me to give to others in meaningful ways. So I am living just as I want, although the days aren't long enough. Otherwise, I'm perfectly content."

Becoming aware of who we are and the foundation for the choices we make allows us to find a better balance in our lives.

Stifling Our Resilience

We live in a society that markets the concept that all pain is bad, to be avoided. It offers easy remedies for headache and colds. From using over-the-counter drugs to alcohol, prescription drugs, and illegal substances, we try our best to shield ourselves from undesirable feelings. Not only pain, but sometimes feelings of restlessness, inadequacy, or unworthiness.

Pain is not always bad. It can serve as a stimulus, to get our attention that something is wrong and needs to be changed. When we block our discomfort, we may block our opportunities to grow. When we mask our feelings, we treat the symptom of the problem, not its cause. In this light, drinking, other drug use, and compulsive behaviors that deaden discomfort end up clipping our wings, cutting us off from our resilient voice.

Often without realizing it, women use alcohol and other drugs to modulate their feelings. For example, they often deal with personal or professional stresses by anesthetizing themselves with alcohol. Other women come home from a full day at work and pour a glass of wine to give them the energy to prepare dinner and make it through the evening. Still others, having worked an eighteen-hour day, use alcohol to shift gears, to counteract the overstimulation of the day. In these and many other ways, women use alcohol to "take the edge off" of situations that could be better dealt with if they learned to sit with the edge and take a different course of action.

Other ways we deplete ourselves of our resilience include overeating and compulsive sexual behaviors, which are used to overcome a feeling of emptiness or unworthiness. Consumerism, the need to buy, to spend, to fill time with shopping, can be another attempt to fill ourselves while actually depleting and diminishing our resources. In all these cases, when we try to run away from ourselves by using something else to fill in a gap, we need to ask why and see if there is a gentler, more accepting way to treat ourselves.

Often we are simply seeking a ritual that signals to us that it is time to relax. At these points a glass of wine or a snack serves to say that we are "off duty." Eating, drinking, and shopping have become symbols that our time now belongs to us.

Some women who have gone on to develop alcoholism or eating disorders can trace the beginning of their difficulty to this seemingly benign behavior, while others have found these behaviors problematic just because they dull the senses and mask the true nature of a problem that needs attention.

With planning we can find better symbols to indicate a shift in gears or way to treat ourselves. A glass of iced juice, a walk after work, an enjoyable book, or some other activity can also symbolize the change in the demands on us.

Understanding What We Need

When we feel the need for "a little something" to relax or reward ourselves, we often seek out familiar, comforting behaviors, such as having a drink or a snack, without asking ourselves what it is we really need. Ask yourself to answer clearly the following questions.

- How often do you feel anxious and in need of something?
- When and why do you usually feel this way?
- What do you usually reach for? A drink? Your credit card? Or do you prowl your kitchen looking for a snack that will fill the void?
- Is one enough, or do you find that you need more than one?
- Afterward, do you feel satisfied, or just numbed?
- Are you concerned about this? Have you noticed that you are drinking more than you think, or spending more than you are comfortable with, or eating more than you need to satisfy your hunger?
- Is anyone else concerned about the choices that you make?
- Have you tried alternatives, such as trying to write out what is bothering you, or exercising, or developing a plan to eliminate the problem you are struggling with? What was the result?

These are the moments when we need to use our resilience, to capitalize upon the inner resources we have developed so that we can truly take care of ourselves by identifying what is wrong and setting about to develop a plan to make it right, or by assessing our needs and finding ways to take care of them that are more balanced.

Please note: If you find yourself unable to change your patterns of drinking, eating, shopping, or other behaviors, or if these cause you concern, be sure to get help. Look in your newspaper or the Yellow Pages for Twelve Step groups or therapists who specialize in your area of concern.

Friends

Friendships are among the most complex and flexible relationships women have and often represent a substantial investment in our lives. Many childhood friendships remain strong into our golden years. If nourished, they can serve as an important source of personal satisfaction and special nurturance. Against the steadily changing backdrop of our lives, as we move, change jobs, marry, divorce, or watch our children grow up and leave home, our friends can provide a source of rootedness, a type of personal history and continuity in an otherwise chaotic life. This is especially true of friends who share our deepest values.

Because they fuel our imagination and allow us to see our potential, our friends can be a source of wings. We may find ourselves attracted to people who live as we would like to live or to those who do what we hope to attain.

Janet told me, "I was thrilled when the teacher of my watercolor workshop asked me for coffee after class. She was the first professional artist I had ever met. Since then, she and I have become good friends and go to museums and exhibits together. She tells me I remind her of herself years ago. I learn so much from our time together."

In the case of difficult families and dark legacies, friends can fill an important place in our lives in helping us heal and develop. We can

131

choose friends that respond to our needs and serve as a new family that can complement or replace the family into which we were born. Our friendships nurture us in many of these essential ways.

Conversely, friendships can also reinforce our dark side. As we recreate the relationship patterns we learned as children, we may associate with individuals who assume familiar but destructive roles. They may be quick to point out our faults, treat us in deprecating ways, or betray our trust. This may be a problem especially for women of overwhelmed resilience, who experienced pain as an inevitable part of relationships. When friendships hurt, it is important to examine them and what is going on. It may be that you need to choose another set of friends who can understand you and contribute to your life in positive ways.

All relationships change and grow. Even good friendships will change with time and require us to adjust or end them. This growth may be very painful as old friendships dissolve. Fortunately, we can rely on our resilience to help us make these changes.

Friends and Our Patterns of Resilience

Friends are yet another window through which we can assess our independence, strengths, and ability to care for ourself. Our friendships reflect our resilience as well as our needs. The people we choose to invite into our lives tell us much about what is happening internally.

A woman with undeveloped resilience may not see what she has to offer in a friendship. She may feel driven to have friends and feel empty and abandoned without them. A woman of self-contained resilience may have few if any friends, as this may be a part of her life which is not developed. A woman with paradoxical resilience may have friends to whom she gives, but from whom she cannot receive in turn. She will pick friends who need to take from others. Stellar women will attract friends who can understand their family history and see them in the context of their present life. A woman whose resilience is overwhelmed has few friends, but may feel drawn to other people who are also full of shame or who can voice the negative feelings she feels about herself. A woman of balanced resilience usually has a blend of friends whom she can draw upon to have her multiple needs met.

What we need in a friend develops over time. Depending on our degree of resilience, we may have many types of friendships and many needs that can be nurtured through them. We will have different needs at different times in our life. In our twenties, for example, we may enjoy joining groups of co-workers at baseball games or concerts. As we meet more of life's challenges and grow more reflective, we may cherish our close women friends who can talk with us one-to-one, especially as we experience such changes as motherhood, divorce, illness, and menopause.

On a day-to-day basis, friends can function as our most intimate relationships where we can be ourselves, share our feelings, and walk away renewed. We may forget that making time for special friends offers an important way of caring for ourselves. The following scenario is typical.

Phyllis left work early to prepare dinner and get the children bathed and in pajamas in time for her to meet Andrea at the movie theater. Just as she finished the last of her preparations, her husband called from the office to say he'd be late. Phyllis called Andrea to cancel their date.

"I can't get away," Phyllis explained, her tears just below the surface. "And anyway, I shouldn't really spend the money."

Later that evening, Phyllis realized she hadn't seen Andrea in three months; it had been six months since she'd seen a movie. Why was it she had no time for herself anymore?

We may tend to think of friendships as a form of recreation, something we can make time for only after all our responsibilities have been met. I encourage women to realize that time spent with good friends can be a way of spending time with what is most important to themselves.

In our conversations with friends, we can give voice to feelings and ideas that we may not otherwise have a chance to express. We can receive support and fresh opinions. In this way, our friends can reinforce our own resilient voice and help us to learn more about ourselves. Our ability to select friends who foster our resilience and self-nurturing is a good indication that we listen to our resilient voice.

Priority Questionnaire

Our resilient voice can help us understand our personal priorities. The ways in which we allocate our time and energy should reflect these priorities, as well as our identity and personal goals. If the center of your life is your career, you should arrange other aspects around it. If you value your family, you should have time to spend with them. If you value your friends, you should see them. If you value your health, you need to make time to exercise and plan healthful meals. If you enjoy theater, music, or art, allowance should be made for those.

Given your resources, you should be able to decide how much should be spent on what you value. The key word is *value*.

Ask your resilient voice to answer the following questions. You might want to spend some time thinking about them before you commit your thoughts to paper.

1. What is the most important area of your life now, the area in which you want to spend the largest amount of your emotional energy (i.e., the energy that it takes to plan, prepare, and follow through).

   - Is this your work life? Are you building a career or finishing school and need to concentrate on this?
   - Is it your family, a new relationship, or managing your home?
   - Is it another personal goal that is most important now?
   - Are you happy about how you spend your emotional energy?
   - Do you need to adjust it?
   - If you do, where could you spend less emotional time?
   - Where do you want to spend more emotional time?

2. Where do you spend most of your physical energy? Is this at work, at home, in school, or on hobbies?

   - Is this satisfying for you, or do you need to make a change here? What could do with less physical energy and what could do with more?
   - How much energy, both emotional and physical, have you allotted for your own personal relaxation, hobbies, or friends?

3. Remember what you did last weekend. (If for some reason that was not a representative weekend, think of another recent one.) Write down your major activities and how much money and time they took.

   - Was this a good balance for you?
   - If you could change this weekend, what changes would you make, keeping in mind the responsibilities that you have?
   - What is your most important free-time activity? Is it seeing friends, reading, cooking, skiing, something else?
   - How much of your time do you allow for this? Is it enough?

4. If you realize that you are not spending time the way you would like to, ask yourself:

   - What gets in the way?
   - Is there a belief that you should not take care of yourself or you don't deserve to have your priorities honored?
   - Do you feel selfish or unentitled if you do?
   - Is this an internalized voice you can identify?
   - Are you unsure of what you would like to do? When you ask yourself, what do you hear? Can you hear your resilient voice speaking and guiding you?
   - Are there too many demands on you? Why is this?
   - Can you use your resilient voice to change these?

- Is there something stopping you? Can you identify whose voice this is?
- Does this need an adjustment? What would you have to give up to have more time for your priorities? What would happen if you did?
- Does your life represent your values, your goals? Why or why not? What changes need to occur to bring your life into line with your values?

Remember that your priorities are important enough for you to work achieve them. Remember, too, that they will change at different points in your life and you should be ready to make the changes you need to accommodate them.

CHAPTER 8

A Woman's Love

Although it was past 2:00 A.M., Jean sat the kitchen table, trying to decide what to do. Her thoughts took the form of an inner dialogue with her resilient voice.

It's no good going on pretending, her resilient voice said, *You ignored Mark's infidelity for months, maybe years. You overlooked all the telltale signs; you saw them, you knew. But seeing him with her tonight, it's all out in the open now.*

I know, but I can't face it, she thought. Frankly, I'm afraid to be alone. I'm thirty-eight. I want what other people have. I enjoy our sex life. I like this beautiful house we can afford with our two salaries. Who knows, maybe he'll even change his thinking about getting married and having children. Is that too much to ask?

Her resilient voice then said, *You need to face the fact that you'll never have what you want with Mark. The choice is yours: leave, or settle for what Mark can give you. Are you really ready to settle for something less than you need?*

Jean paused as she let this last thought sink in. No, she had to admit, she was not ready to compromise her dream of a deep and loving relationship. She resolved to end her relationship with Mark then and there. Much to her amazement, instead of panic or sorrow, she felt only immense relief. She knew that it was the right choice.

How did I ever get myself into this mess? she wondered. How did I learn to ask for so little?

We all have different expectations about what love is and what a relationship should be. For some, love is primarily giving; for others, primarily receiving. Some experience love as a great tempestuous passion, and some find a lifelong relationship built on understanding and companionship. How we think of love, what we feel when we experience love, and how we give love are unique to each of us.

Whatever our experience, we have a primary need to love and be loved. Although some of us may try to deny or close off this part of ourselves, love is an essential part of our humanity. While each of us may have our own ideas of the perfect partner or love affair, the need for love is universal.

Why then do so many search so long for what others seem to find so easily? What sort of luck or special knowledge do successful couples possess? We may not realize that our search for love is thwarted less by external factors—our appearance or where we work or the way we talk—than by internal factors—our ability to risk vulnerability or to balance what we give with what we receive. Also important are the type of partner we select, how we expect love to be expressed, and whether, like Jean, we may try to settle for what will not ultimately give us what we want.

To find the love we need, we must confront the internal factors that keep us from fulfilling and meaningful relationships. We can do this best by means of our resilient voice. It can help us become conscious of what we want and need, and summon the strength and self-love to act on that knowledge.

Understanding How We Love

The poet Rainer Maria Rilke described love as the embracing of two solitudes. This means two whole beings who come together but do not lose who they are individually. Ideally, in loving another we continue to love ourselves, even while we embrace and care deeply for our partner.

Love depends upon our ability to achieve this balance between independence—our wholeness—and vulnerability—our willingness to embrace. As we have seen, this is what resilience is all about, the balance of self-regard and regard for others. We need to decide how much of ourselves to yield in a relationship and how much to retain, how much to give and how much to ask that others give us.

Jean was startled at the sense of excitement and self-love she felt as she contemplated living alone for the first time in seven years. She said, "In letting Mark take care of me, I allowed myself to be held hostage to his whims without realizing it. I lost myself. Once I planned to leave, I began to feel alive again. I realized I had been so tense trying to hold onto something that was not real. Now I had to take care of myself instead of depending on someone else to do this for me. Framing the situation this way, I suddenly began to feel strong enough to do it."

Many women with undeveloped resilience experience a similar dilemma when they fall in love. Like Jean, they tend to be reluctant to take charge of their lives. They look for relationships that will provide them a sense of definition, seeking fulfillment from their partner. When we consider ourselves to be someone else's "other half" we can never feel whole.

Women of undeveloped resilience often enjoy traditional roles as the loyal helpmate of their partner, continuing in their adult love relationships the same childhood pattern of turning power over to others. To correct this, they need to find a way to develop their own self-definition and self-worth and to believe in their power and ability to attend to their own needs.

A woman with balanced resilience, by contrast, already adept at recognizing both her strengths and neediness, will be better able to ride the ebb and flow of relationships. She knows that finding what she really wants may require her to take chances and that she has the resilience to risk being vulnerable. More than women of other resilience patterns, she is liable to be successful at the give-and-take relationships require. She tends to have the wisdom to look for love in places where it is likely to be fulfilled and not to ask too much from love. It is not uncommon for these women to have had good models on which to pattern their own relationships.

Women of self-contained resilience styles frequently spend so much time and energy on their careers, they may believe they have no time for relationships. That is the excuse, at any rate. It is more often true that they experience trouble in relationships and so minimize the role intimate relationships play in their life. Just as they used their competence to shield their vulnerability in childhood and to survive difficult circumstances, so they continue to distance themselves from the vulnerability of deep relationships.

Women of self-contained resilience can benefit from the recognition that risk-taking and mastery are part of who they are and that they can draw on these qualities in all areas of their lives. This appreciation of their strengths may allow them to use this skill on their own behalf in risking intimacy.

Moriah was a successful lawyer with the same firm as her husband. In many ways they had the perfect relationship, as each fully supported the other's career. Sometimes this meant that they lived in different cities for months at a time, seeing each other only on weekends.

This carefully maintained balance was upset when Moriah realized she was pregnant. She came to counseling to work out her feelings about the situation.

"I have always wanted children at some point in my life, but this has always been an abstract desire," said Moriah. "I'm not ready to be a mother. And it's not only the idea that I would have to take on such a new and foreign role, but that I would need to depend on Stan in so many new ways. That is the terrifying part for me. Stan and I are companions, good friends, but always independent of each other. A child would change all this."

This, she said, was the reason she was planning to arrange an abortion. The difficulty was that her pregnancy had made her very aware of how much she wanted to have a child.

We talked about her fear and about the other times she had been afraid of important changes in her life. "How did you deal with those?" I asked.

"Sheer moxie," she said, smiling proudly. "I've taken risks all my life. The more afraid I was, the more determined I was to see it through."

"And now?"

"I guess I'm terrified enough to talk to Stan about having the baby and what I'll need from him."

As it turned out, Moriah was amazed at her husband's response. Later she reported, "Stan said he would support my motherhood as strongly as he had supported my career. And he's been true to his word. We became even closer during my pregnancy. We began sharing the more personal sphere of hopes and fantasies that there never seemed time or reason to share before. And since the baby, this has become an even larger piece of our lives."

Women of stellar resilience similarly have trouble letting down their guard. It is hard for them to believe that love can be different from what they experienced as a child. They have been betrayed before and have learned that trust is not to be given lightly. For this reason, women of stellar resilience may unwittingly test any who proclaim love for them. This testing can take many forms, from accusations of infidelity, to hurling charges that their partner doesn't truly love them.

Lori has been prone to jealousy in relationships throughout her life. She said, "Somehow I've always had difficulty believing that someone could love me, even though I love him. So I'm always looking for ways to judge my partner's love. It's no surprise that Roger and I had problems, all of which I seemed to blame on myself.

"The worst is that Roger travels extensively on business. Every trip, it seemed, I'd call and find he wasn't where he told me he'd be. He'd tell me he'd be back at the hotel by 7:30, and I'd call and there would be no answer. I would get so angry and upset, we'd have a terrible fight when he got home, just like my parents used to.

"The last fight we had Roger yelled, 'You won't *let* me love you!' Something clicked with this. I realized he was right. I was afraid to let him love me. Instead of looking for his love, I kept searching for his rejection. It's started some fundamental changes in the way I understand our relationship and my reactions in particular."

Women like Lori need to learn to use their resilience when they love to give them the guidance and the courage to love without the expectation of pain. In doing this, they will be able to trust intimacy enough to allow others to get closer to them. Learning to love themselves and others unreservedly is another step in their already defined path of growth.

Paradoxically resilient women are unable to achieve a balance between their vulnerability and their strengths. They may section off their ability to love, keeping it apart from their self-identity. If so, they will fail to derive satisfaction and personal meaning from it. Or they may feel very confident in their ability to love another but not in their own lovability. These women need to learn to reconcile the two halves of loving: the giving and receiving. Here an inner dialogue can help to remind them of their many different needs and abilities and achieve a better balance in their resilience.

Women of overwhelmed resilience will tend to carry on a tradition of the unhappy love experienced as children. These women have learned that love involves pain and that being in love may involve rejection, abandonment, humiliation, and the intensity of "making up." They need to learn how to love and give, while protecting themselves and risking only what they can afford to lose.

The Love Around Us

Our understanding of love is formulated in childhood, beginning in infancy with our unconditional love of ourselves and those who cared for us. Such love was free of judgments and represented the basis of our self-acceptance, the deepest of those elements that root us and provide the basis of our identity.

This kind of self-love is evident in an infant who is trying to walk. Fall as she may, she keeps going, delighted to accomplish this movement on two legs. Despite collisions with tables, tears, and pressure from adults, she accomplishes this task with an inevitable feeling of satisfaction, delight, and mastery.

Unfortunately, the love we perceive as a child may be very different from the unconditional love we initially give ourselves and those around us. Our caretakers' feelings for us and for each other may be more circumscribed and expressed only in judging terms, even abuse. It is these first experiences that teach us what love is—a joyful experience or a painful one, an impossible ideal or a commonplace treasure.

These experiences form beliefs that will guide our actions in adult-hood, unless we recognize these patterns and choose and alter them.

If we believe that love should be joyful, as woman of balanced resilience may feel, then we will seek to fulfill this belief. Karen came from a loving home with its fair share of ups and downs. She said, "My dad was the real old-fashioned type. He wasn't long on praise, but every once in a while he'd show up with a bouquet of flowers for Mom, or buy her some special gift. It was fun to watch the two of them at these moments. I think we kids enjoyed them as much as they did. Occasionally our folks would argue, and the world seemed upside down, but they would work it out. You could see the respect they had for each other and the effort each made to please to the other. That's what I want in my relationships: love based on respect. I am lucky that I had such a clear idea of what love can be. It's the standard by which I evaluate my own relationships."

Karen was fortunate to have an example of a relationship in which struggles and conflict, as well as love and respect, were dealt with in productive ways. As a result, Karen will be able to experience conflict and work to resolve it, rather than fearing it or responding in abusive and counterproductive ways.

In other families, children see only the pain of adult relationships. Consequently, they grow up to believe that love should be painful. As adults they may unconsciously seek out painful love experiences, such as those often encountered by women of overwhelmed resilience.

Totie's mother and stepfather, both alcoholics, argued on a regu-lar basis. From her earliest years Totie witnessed her parents' terrible arguments, which frequently erupted into physical violence, verbal abuse, and humiliation. To this day Totie has vivid memories of see-ing her stepfather hit her mother, spit at her, and call her a slut and a whore. Later she would hear her mother tearfully forgiving her step-father and the sounds of lovemaking. This type of family teaches bonding through anger and abuse. It demonstrates that violence is something deserved that then can be readily done away with and even serve as a prelude to sex. It teaches shaming and attaches shame to love and sexuality.

Without realizing it, Totie concluded that lovemaking and humiliation are all part of the intimacy ritual. As she matures Totie may begin to act on these beliefs about love. If she is loyal to the beliefs of her family, she will be susceptible to reenacting its cycle of abuse and battery in her own relationships until she learns to use her resilience to love differently.

Natalie grew up believing that love was unattainable. "It was like a self-fulfilling prophecy," said Natalie. "My mom was always looking, never finding. At the end of every relationship, she'd buy a big carton of ice cream, sit me down and say, 'Looks like it's just you and me, kid.'

"I spent years as a young woman looking for men and buying ice cream. If I'd spent more time on responding to my own needs and less time hunting, I would have found Justin sooner."

Being attracted to someone who cannot love and blaming one's own lack of desirability is also a pattern learned in childhood. Some women stay in relationships with unavailable partners as a way to unconsciously prove that they are not lovable.

Kim felt this way. "When my parents divorced, I was fourteen," said Kim, "My father disappeared. He never called me and I didn't see him for twelve years. I've been trying to find him ever since by dating older men who can somehow never decide to leave their wife, or never decide if they really want a relationship. Until recently, I always thought it was me, that I wasn't worth loving. But I've been having some good talks with myself and with a therapist, and I'm beginning to see that it's the choices I make and not who I am that create these relationships. I'm working on changing my choices."

Changing Our Childhood Patterns

Some women look outside their family's patterns and hold onto other dreams. These women rely on their wings to find models that can answer their needs for healthy relationships.

Lily realized early on that life had to be different for her than it had been for her mother. Her father died when she was nine and her mother, then only thirty-five, became severely depressed. Lily was the oldest of the four children and helped to raise the rest. "I was determined that I would never act like my mother, that I would never just love once and then endure a living death.

"I always remembered my father, his laughter, and the good times we had, and knew that feeling good could be part of life," she said. Lily used her own outgoing personality to open some doors for her. "I dated boys with close-knit families that looked good to me. Their mothers were energetic; their fathers were available. I wanted to be part of that," said Lily.

"In high school I fell for George, or I should say George's family. By being with them I learned how healthy families live. They were affectionate and fun. I dated George throughout high school and into college. We broke up my sophomore year, but I feel I owe him a great deal. His family showed me the kind of love that I like to think would have been in my family if my father had lived."

Our first impressions of love are deeply ingrained, hidden away from our conscious mind and the decisions we make. As a result, it takes a special effort to recognize our expectations about love and the patterns we have unconsciously carried with us. Once we recognize them, however, we can begin to change them. It may be that we must risk unpatriotic thoughts and behaviors to achieve what we need, a task we can accomplish through dialogue with our resilient voice.

Tia was married and deeply in love with her husband. She originally began counseling because her husband was about to leave her. The problem was that he loved her but could no longer stand their intensely painful arguments. Tia came from an abusive family and learned how to give and receive love in painful ways. Her husband felt that the price of her love was too high. He loved her, but he loved himself as well.

At first she couldn't understand what he meant. "I thought, that's how adults behave. No one's perfect. No one gets along all the time," said Tia. "So we had fights. I'd make it up later. Why wasn't that enough?

"I didn't realize how out of line my actions were. I'd storm through the house, break dishes, use language I'd never think of in a normal conversation. I didn't realize how much it hurt him and how it had damaged our relationship, until he threatened to leave. Now I'm learning how to express my anger in different, more reasonable ways. It's not easy. I have to unlearn some very ingrained behaviors. But I love him, and I'm trying to learn that love doesn't have to hurt.

"My most successful trick is to write out my anger before I even talk to him, allowing my resilient voice to provide a more balanced perspective. That way, I don't dump my raw anger on my husband. Then we can talk about it and settle the situation. It may not be easy all the time, but it's worth it to work it out—peacefully."

If you have had trouble with relationships in the past, you can begin to examine what it is that has kept you from the relationships you need. Is there a self-defeating pattern of intimacy that you learned as a child that interferes with your relationships? Are you able to identify your needs and communicate them to your partner? Because our expectations are derived from what we already know, they may keep us within the narrow range of our experience, limiting our choices.

Our resilience can help us in discovering new choices. We can learn how to overcome the shame we may have attached to our need for love, or, like Tia, to love ourselves enough to make difficult changes so that our relationships can begin to provide the nurturing and support we need.

How Love Was Shown

Our families teach us how to demonstrate love. As adults, we look for these signals. If we are unaware of them or their importance to us, we may be disappointed when others do not demonstrate their love in these particular ways. We may also misinterpret others' signals. If our family is stoic and feelings are rarely shown, then reticence will be the norm for us. If we come from a demonstrative family, then effusiveness will be our norm.

In some families love is present but unavailable. Rosa knew her father loved her, but he was an angry man with a bitter temper. "I'm not sure who suffered more from his inability to show his gentle feelings for us," she said sadly.

Another problem may occur if our temperament is out of sync with our family's. If you were a shy child who craved privacy in an effusive family, you would certainly have felt uncomfortable. If you were a sensitive person who craved holding and cuddling, you may have been at odds in a stoic family.

Take a couple of moments to relax. Have paper and a pen handy. Now think back to your childhood. Using your resilient voice, answer the following questions. Write your responses.

- Think about how you knew you were loved as a child. What conclusions did you draw about how parents demonstrate their love for a child? Did you receive your parents' time and attention? Did being loved mean that you were provided with three meals a day, clothes, and shelter? Was your birthday celebrated with a party each year? Did your parents pay for your college education?

- What were the small gestures that meant you were loved? Were you kissed and hugged, or spanked to make you behave? Did you get love notes in your lunchbox?

- Do you feel your family was successful in demonstrating their love in ways that were satisfying and meaningful for you?

- Do you still continue to show love in this way?

- If you are in a relationship, does your partner know that this is how you love?

- Are you content with showing love in this way?

- Would you like to change?

- What specific changes would you make?

- What, if anything, stops you?

If there are changes you want to make, put these answers aside and go back to them in a little while, perhaps in a month or so.

Then do this exercise again and see if you have made any of the changes you wanted.

Falling in Lust

Sexuality evokes many complex and deep emotions that we may not even be aware of. They may be based on beliefs taught us years ago, such as that women do not enjoy sex, or that to have sexual relations outside the context of a long-term (if not lifelong) relationship is wrong. These beliefs may be at odds with the times in which we live or our values in other areas of life. In today's atmosphere of sexual freedom, we may find it difficult to know how to recognize what we want or how to ask for it. More importantly, we may feel shy or may not know to speak up about issues of safety in intimate relationships.

Despite the so-called sexual revolution, many women have difficulty in relationships because they have been taught that it is wrong for a woman to have strong sexual feelings. While strong feelings of affection are permissible, strong sexual feelings are not—even after marriage. To compensate for this, some women attach loving feelings to relationships which are significantly less deep or meaningful to them. This can be confusing to themselves and their partner.

Marissa was telling her brother excitedly about the new love of her life. He responded by asking her a devastating question: "When *haven't* you been in love with the person you're dating?"

"I realized I didn't have a good answer for him," Marissa said. "I usually feel that I'm in love with whoever I am seeing. I could say I always pick winners who are easy to love, but I know this is not true. The truth is, I feel so empty inside that I need someone to fill me up. I do this through sex. And I convince myself that I'm in love with whoever I'm dating, so it's okay. I know I'm not committed to them."

Without understanding our sexual feelings, we may seek satisfaction in self-defeating ways. Consider the situation of two women competing for the same man. Both may try to bed him, avowing their commitment and love to him, while he remains detached and seemingly ambivalent about whom he prefers. Yet if either woman could step outside of the situation for a moment, she might wonder whether someone so unavailable is truly desirable. If honest, she might admit that it is the quest that excites her and not the man.

Other women feel they must block off their feelings if they are to adhere to societal and familial norms and mores. They may suppress their sexuality or seek to be punished or hurt because of it. They may unconsciously seek out partners who are judgmental of their sexual needs or uninterested in them sexually.

Ginger's husband would withdraw whenever she initiated any sexual activity whether kissing or lovemaking. "It was devastating for me," said Ginger. "I needed sex. And just when it seemed that we would make love, Max would close down and turn away. I would be left hanging, and so I would masturbate. But this felt empty."

Still others seek only to pleasure their partner without receiving pleasure themselves. They deny this part of themselves. Mandy found receiving pleasure difficult and married someone who had difficulty in encouraging her sexually.

"Our sex life is perfunctory," she said. "Somehow we've managed to have three children, but sex doesn't mean much to me."

Your sexual self is an integral part of who you are. Use your inner voice to discover and keep up a dialogue about this very important part of you. The more you know about yourself sexually the more you will be able to share with your partner, and the more enjoyable your sexual encounters will be. You deserve this. Claim your sexuality by becoming more friendly with this part of you.

Meagan, whose resilience was undeveloped, found that taking responsibility for herself as a sexual adult allowed her to grow. She said, "I had been brought up in a very traditional and religious family. I somehow always felt that life for me would be just the same as for my mother.

"Then I graduated from college and found myself living away from home in a strange city. I'd meet men who were attractive, but I didn't have a clue how to date. I didn't have my church or my family to give me guidelines, only myself. So I became the resident expert on what I needed. I learned to talk to myself, and most of all to listen to what my impulses were telling me was right. The added benefit is that I can be very clear with my partner about all aspects of our relationship, including sex. He appreciates this and has learned to respond in kind. I think it's made the relationship much stronger."

Making Sex Safe

Being safe while being sexual is a major challenge today. It requires women to be assertive and to take responsibility for their own well-being. This means learning to do things that would have been considered unnecessary a few years ago, such as carrying condoms or using vaginal condoms to protect ourselves from both unwanted pregnancy and sexually transmitted diseases. Being safe also means learning to insist that a potential lover take an HIV test before the relationship becomes sexual. This requires planning and alters the level of spontaneity in the relationship. These steps are difficult for some women to take, particularly if they have trouble speaking up or if they have abdicated most of their power to their partner.

Speaking Up

Use your resilient voice to speak up for yourself and to make your concerns known, particularly in terms of what will protect you from unsafe sex. If this is difficult at first, rehearse how to broach difficult topics, such as requesting that your partner use a condom every time you have intercourse. Here are some techniques that might be helpful:

- Try writing out what you would like to say. When you are comfortable with the words, you can send your partner a note.
- Talk into a tape recorder to hear your voice and to acknowledge what it is you need from your partner.
- Talk to friends about how they discuss sexual subjects with their partners.
- Talk to your partner. Try to fight your awkwardness, embar-

rassment, or annoyance and find the words that convey your feelings.

Find the method that works for you, and use it until you are more comfortable. Realize that you are entitled to bring up the topic of safe sex more than once. Your life depends on it.

New Directions

Anita always came back glowing from her regional sales meetings. She would inevitably find the perfect man, a star-crossed lover who was perfectly suited for her but who, tragically, was married to someone else. The affair would begin intensely and then gradually wind down as some tragic flaw was discovered, such as the fact that his wife was pregnant, or that he was also seeing someone else. "I'm compulsive about everything else, why not how I fall in love?" shrugged Anita. "Maybe I'm just an intensity junkie.

"But something is changing. Just this last trip I heard myself thinking, I'm getting too old for this. I need to settle down and find a man that's real—read *available.*

"In the past I used to hear a voice saying, 'Take what you can get. You can cultivate your garden later. You're in a hurry now.' For the last ten years, this has been fine. But this time I realized, now is later. I'm almost thirty and haven't had a serious relationship with an available partner since leaving college.

"I recognized my father's voice as the one telling me I was in a hurry. In many ways I'm very much like him, the son he never had. I'm aggressive and take what I want. Like me, he was in sales, always making a deal, never home, always traveling."

Anita realized that this style of love was no longer satisfying to her. She wanted more from a relationship than just excitement and intensity, and her inner voice let her know that it was time for a change. But how to change? Anita saw that she was afraid to make a commitment to a partner, something she had no problem doing in her career. "It's time to shift gears and bring some of my strengths to work for me in relationships," she said.

In the process of finding our own voice on the issue of love, we may hear other voices within us. We may hear a voice that says women are there to please their husband or women can never love their mate as much as they love their children. There may be voices that state our inherent unlovability. Allowing ourselves to hear and identify these different viewpoints allows us to move beyond them and no longer be trapped by self-defeating beliefs.

Confronting Problems in Relationships

Frequently our identity is tied to our major love relationship. This makes it terribly painful and complicated when we need to question whether this relationship is right for us or if it would be better to end it. To entertain such a question, we need to separate ourselves a little and try to be objective about a very subjective process.

All relationships are about give and take, for they must accommodate the needs of two people. So in effect, every relationship is a compromise, because to make such an arrangement work, there needs to be an adjustment of expectations that allows room for each partner's good points and foibles. This means learning to accept less than the ideal in many areas, while striving to have an overall balance that is nurturing.

Knowing when you are in love requires you to have an inner knowledge of your own needs and feelings so you can know if these are being fulfilled and if you are happy. From time to time we need to ask ourselves, Am I still happy? Am I still fulfilled? If I pull back a little do I like what I see? What can I do to make it better for my partner and me? Here, instead of following our heart, we need to see our situation clearly and communicate it to our partner. In this process, our resilience can prove a formidable ally.

Suzi, a woman of balanced resilience, was irresistibly wooed by Jeff. The fact that he had two sons didn't greatly bother her as they lived with their mother in Texas, and they seemed nice enough.

The situation soon changed, however. A year after their marriage, just as Suzi was expecting her first child, Jeff's oldest son decided to live with them. Six months later, the second son moved up. In less than two years of marriage, Suzi found herself caring for teenage boys and an infant girl.

"I was afraid to leave, but I felt so taken advantage of," said Suzi. "Jeff and the boys kept so busy with guy things, like fishing and basketball, that I felt abandoned. Here I'd taken a year's leave to be a full-time mother to my baby, and I felt like a housekeeper and chauffeur."

One night Suzi was so angry that she sat down and wrote Jeff a farewell letter. "I spelled out everything I felt was wrong about our relationship and the way he and the boys treated me and our daughter. I explained that I was leaving and wouldn't come back until he could assure me that things would be different.

"As I reread it, a question came to me, How can you leave when you've never told him any of this before? How is he supposed to know how you feel? It isn't right to leave before telling him face to face.

"And it was true. I'd been so involved in trying to be the good sport, I'd never honestly confronted Jeff. In fact, I'd never really thought out my feelings, point by point. I didn't leave. Instead, I used the letter to help me talk to Jeff. To my relief, he was willing to make changes. I discovered Jeff felt overwhelmed at having the boys again and guilty that he couldn't spend more time with our daughter. So we made arrangements to have the boys visit their mother over the summer so we could have time for the three of us.

"It would have been so easy to walk out, if I hadn't listened to what was bothering me and found a way to tell Jeff."

When Love Goes Wrong

When relationships begin to experience serious trouble, it is difficult to tell if it is time to go, or if it is time to work harder. If we try to reconcile, are we settling for less than we need in our relationship? Or are we responsibly working through the conflict to make the relationship stronger and better? In judging our own situation, we must realize that there is an important difference between compromising, which represents a hopeful, reciprocal stance, and settling, a static position that offers us few options.

When her husband had an affair, Helen fought to hold onto their relationship. "I was terribly hurt, but I loved him," she said. "I loved him enough to fight for him. We have problems, but I think we can resolve them. What matters most is that our caring for one another is still there."

At other times we may need a break, perhaps a temporary cooling off period before we can recommit to the relationship. Or we may realize we are just not willing to do the work needed to save a relationship and that we need to end it because that the quality and satisfaction have diminished.

Maxine wondered if it just wasn't time to leave. Her children were in high school, and her husband was now more demanding than ever. Demanding, but not sexual. Sex seemed to have stopped years ago. "We're like two railroad cars, each on a separate track," said Maxine. "We pass and wave, but never touch. I've thought about trying again. But I'm tired; we've been here too many times before. And nothing that I can do ever seems to make it better for long."

The major difference between Helen and Maxine is that Helen is still committed to a relationship that has potential for further growth. Maxine, on the other hand, has lost her commitment, because previous solutions were never able to address the core issue.

Abusive Love

While commitment can give us our wings by defining our hope for what our love relationship can give us, commitment alone does not prevent serious problems, such as those that occur in abusive relationships. Physically and verbally abusive relationships are often about power and control. Even healthy women can be swept up in this cycle when they begin to give their power to another. They begin to hear only the voice of their partner and tune out their own inner voice.

In a typical scenario, women are attracted to partners who sweep them off their feet. "Ed was the most romantic man I ever met. We had a whirlwind courtship," said Denise. "So two weeks after we were married, when he beat me for changing the TV channel, I really thought I had done something wrong. Especially when he later apologized for it. But gradually the beatings came more often. I blamed myself. There was always a good reason, it seemed.

"When I got a promotion that caused us to move, Ed took a cut in pay and blamed me for it. He became even more jealous and possessive. The beatings continued. Finally came the moment of truth. One morning I sat crying in the bathroom after an all-night battle. I caught a glimpse of myself, my face red and contorted, a bruise forming on my chin. I said out loud to my reflection, 'What in the world are you doing here?'

"In that moment I realized that I had been taking care of Ed and the relationship at the expense of my own well-being. Now it was time to begin taking care of myself. I found an apartment and told Ed I was going. I still see him on weekends so he won't get too angry, and I pay for his apartment. But I am finding the strength to separate and just take care of myself."

Whatever our resilience pattern, our own emerging voice contains an inner wisdom. It can help us decide when what we have is enough or too little, when we need protection, or when we can trust our partner enough to risk intimacy. In the end, our ability to love our partner and to build a fulfilling relationship will always depend on our ability to love ourselves and to maintain a healthy and fulfilling relationship with our resilient self.

Love and Resilience

If you and your partner are experiencing serious problems, don't avoid them, pretending they don't exist. Use your resilient voice to help you answer the following questions.

- What keeps you in the relationship?
- Do you have a personal commitment to continue the relationship?
- Are you more guided by fear of being on your own, or by fear of your partner, than by love and commitment to the relationship?
- Have you grown in this relationship?
- Do you feel that there is potential for you to continue to grow?

- Have you been in this difficult place before? If so, what did you do?
- Was that the right choice? Will that solution work again? Will something else work?
- What is the nature of the problems? Does their solution require a fundamental change in who you are? In your partner? In the relationship?
- What is the nature of the compromises you have made or need to make to continue the relationship? Are they balanced against the quality and satisfaction you derive from the relationship? Are these compromises too much?

Please note: If you are involved in an abusive relationship, seek professional help. Every year thousands of women suffer serious injury or death as a result of domestic violence. There are many organizations and therapists who specialize in domestic violence and can offer both emergency and long-term help. Nothing can be accomplished in a relationship as long as you are unsafe.

_____

CHAPTER 9

Parenting and Resilience

A bumper sticker I saw once summed it up: *I can handle any crisis: I have children.* Indeed, no other normal life experience demands as much of us—physically, emotionally, mentally—as parenting.

Whatever our pattern of resilience, motherhood requires us to grow in new ways, virtually on a daily basis. It involves problem solving, setting aside old standards, and learning new, often difficult, lessons. Out of the many possible approaches to child rearing, we need to find a style that meets our own standards and requirements. We need to contact our deepest beliefs and act upon them, even, at times, in the face of criticism.

Keeping Perspective

The process of parenting is much like a fun-house mirror, enlarging our flaws and faults at times, but also magnifying our strengths and resources. To a large degree, it depends which we choose to see. Through the eyes of our child, we may see a new image of ourselves as all-powerful, larger than life. For many of us, it is not easy to recognize ourselves in this role as the one in charge, responsible for important, even critical, decisions about the welfare and environment of this vulnerable being, our child. We may feel overwhelmed and unequal to the demands of our responsibilities. Here our resilient voice can act as a guide.

157

It is hard to always bring our best to parenting. When we are over-burdened with responsibilities, our children's needs may seem just one more set of demands. We often lose our perspective about what is of lasting importance, both to ourselves and our children.

"Those years when my kids were young were insane," Daphne told me." I was trying to keep house, raise three children, and handle the bookkeeping for my husband's business. No matter what I did, I felt guilty. What I felt worst about, however, was not having time for my kids.

"It took me a while to figure what to do about it, but the answer came when I began to look at each day through their eyes. What did the kids care if I patched those pants today or next week, or if they ate sandwiches off napkins instead of plates? Some afternoons I'd just put aside the bookkeeping and go for a walk in the rain with them. It meant I sat up past 11:00 P.M. catching up on the books some nights, but I felt centered, not off-kilter like before. Every night when I went to bed, my to-do list was just as long as when I'd gotten up in the morning, but if I'd made time for my kids, it was enough."

More than fulfilling the daily tasks of raising our children, par-enting requires us to confront ourselves, past and present. We meet our past in myriad places and on many levels as we reexperience our own childhood through our child's. Motherhood brings us back to our deepest beliefs, reaffirms our roots, and yields new discoveries about our early years. At the same time, we see in our children new beginnings, new hope. Helping them to develop and prepare for the future before them, we remember our own belief in life's possibilities and so rediscover our wings.

This same process may bring a measure of sadness, self-doubt, and even despair. No mother has not regretted some action or word. For those who struggle to redefine motherhood in the wake of a diffi-cult childhood, this is an especially painful aspect of parenting. Here our resilience can play an important role, not only in providing guid-ance and support through the daily tasks of mothering, but through its deeper perspective. It allows us to use our mothering experiences to understand the lessons of our own childhood. It can bring us to a new realization of who and why we are. It can alter the way we live our lives and the lives we create for our children.

The Challenges of Mothering

Little prepares us for the long hours, physical drain, and emotional seesaw that comes with parenting. Add to that the fact that the majority of today's mothers lack the help and support from extended families that were the norm as little as a generation or two ago. These changes have made parenting an often isolating and difficult experience for many women.

Yet it is not the sheer difficulty of the tasks involved in parenting that causes us the most discomfort, but our expectations, the lens through which we view and evaluate our actions. Trying to be a super-mom—to be patient with our children, cook delicious and nutritious meals, have a sky-rocketing career, and look gorgeous at night for our partner—is a sure way to be dissatisfied with all we try to accomplish.

Standards of good parenting are showered on us from many sources. With our societal focus on pathology rather than resilience, mothers are often unfairly blamed for the problems of their children. If a child steals, we may read in a newspaper that her mother worked the night shift as a nurse, leaving her unsupervised. What is not said is that the mother single-handedly supports her family. Many women are deserted by their children's father and receive no support.

Or consider the messages to mothers in books such as *Toxic Parents,* or at the opposite extreme, the images of television and movie mothers, who remain calm, loving, beautiful, and in complete control no matter what. We are bound to evaluate our abilities by these yardsticks and to blame ourselves for all the problems, great and small, that occur in our children's lives. The trouble with this equation is that it gives us too much responsibility without enough real power to make needed changes.

Even those from whom we expect the most support, our friends and family, even our spouse, may be unaware of or insensitive to our needs. Perhaps without meaning to, they may criticize our choices. At this vulnerable time, their inability to lend the support we need may seem the cruelest betrayal of all.

The Critic Within

Our most relentless expectations, however, may come from within. "I'm not the mother I wanted to be," complained Adrienne. "I have looked forward to this time for twenty years and imagined just how it would be. I wanted to give my daughter what my mother, who was manic-depressive, could not. I wanted to be available to her, responsive to her needs. I didn't know I'd be so tired or have so little patience. I know I should allow her to do things on her own, but she's two and is so slow. It takes an hour for her to get through breakfast. I can't get anything done. Her temper tantrums make me break down in tears."

Many mothers like Adrienne equate being a good parent with being a "perfect" parent. If they have rejected the models of their own upbringing, it is especially difficult for them to develop realistic expectations of themselves or to understand the limits of acceptable behavior. They may be more prone to believe in the idealized images they see in the media and social models around them. It is easy to understand how, with such self-expectations, they never seem to measure up.

Whatever vision we may have had about how we would be as a mother, few of us find that the vision matches reality. In many ways, the reality of motherhood exceeds our expectations in the satisfactions, joys, and rewards that caring for our child can give. In many other ways, however, the reality may be far less than our desires. This is because in fantasy, we can dictate how life will be—where we will live, our relationships, our health, our income. Unfortunately, we cannot dictate reality.

"I'm very traditional," states Maureen. "I see all the trouble kids get into today, and I know it's because they don't have anyone who pays attention to them, who cares what they do after school, who knows who their friends are or what movies they watch. Joe and I agreed I'd stay home and be a regular mom. Bake cookies, be a den mother. That was before the cost of living made it impossible for us to get along on one salary. It broke my heart when I realized I'd have to work full time and not be there when the boys came home from school."

Having to compromise our expectations and intentions can make us feel tremendous guilt. This can leave us vulnerable to doubts about whether what we do is effective or to feelings that we can never do enough. The effect is that we always feel dissatisfied and at war within ourselves. A woman already wrestling with feelings of shame and inadequacy is particularly susceptible to this. The result is painful for both mother and child.

Through our resilience, we can transform these negative messages and recognize what it is we have to give, rather than to define our mothering by what we want to give but can't. Janice struggled with this.

"When my husband walked out on me and Sabrina, I thought I was in a dream," said Janice. "It was someone else's life, not mine. How could he do that? We had talked forever about our life together, the four children we would raise, the home we'd have, and the cultural advantages we'd give our children. Suddenly, this beautiful dream was in ruins.

"I don't believe in divorce. I don't believe in putting my own needs above commitment, especially to a family. But what could I do? How could I live up to the promises I'd made to myself about my daughter's childhood?

"Fortunately I realized that I didn't have to do it alone. I became more active in my temple and developed friends among families with the same traditional values as I have. Sabrina belongs to Girl Scouts, and we've gone on camp outs and do a lot of the things I used to do with my brothers and sisters.

"It's not the same as having a real father and brothers and sisters, like I did. But I'm beginning to see that my daughter will have many of the same good memories from childhood that I had. It's a different childhood for her than the one I wanted, but I'm still able to share the most important things. I am grateful for that."

Rather than concentrating on what couldn't be, Janice refused to become trapped in grieving for her losses and concentrated instead on the valuable experiences she could give her daughter. As Janice learned, it is easy to focus on what we can't provide or what we can't be, yet our resilience can show us another perspective. It can tell us that spending our time and energy on feeling guilty detracts from what we give our children. By focusing instead on the gifts and opportunities we can provide, we free ourselves to make the most of what we have to offer.

Loving Ourselves

To teach our children to love themselves, we demonstrate our love for them. We strive to be patient and accepting of them, loving them even in the midst of their mistakes and wrongdoing. That is only half of what we need to do to teach our children self-love; we must also love ourselves. This means making room for our own mistakes as we make room for theirs and learning that progress, not perfection, is the goal. Modeling patience with ourselves teaches it to our children.

Casey was a bright and active six-year-old when his tantrums at school became so disruptive that his mother was called for a conference. His teacher explained that Casey had tantrums when his clay figures fell apart or he made a mistake in his drawings and couldn't erase them. "I'm so stupid! I can't do anything right!" he'd yell and knock the work materials to the floor.

When the teacher told this to his mother, she winced. "I know where he gets it," she said. "From me. I'm pretty hard on myself when I make a mistake." His mother realized that as much as she complimented her son and praised his efforts, he also heard her anger at her own mistakes. It wasn't how she acted toward him, but how she accepted her own frustrations, that he had used as his model.

When we can accept ourselves, faults and all, with self-love and respect, we demonstrate an important aspect of our resilience. When we pick up and start again after a defeat, or acknowledge failure and make another attempt, we as well as our children gain a valuable lesson.

Establishing Priorities

The first step to being a good parent is to set good parenting as a clear priority. Doing so means we choose to see ourselves in this role and value it as a central part of our life. We make a commitment to devote time and energy to it. It establishes a reference point for how we will evaluate ourselves and the choices we make.

Being a good mother does not mean that you are never ambivalent about your responsibilities or even about your children. It does not mean that you don't daydream about a life without children, being able to sleep through the night, or having greater financial freedom or more peace of mind. Any love relationship has moments in which we question and then recommit. This is to be expected.

Spending time with your resilient voice to recognize what really counts is the first step in learning how to be the parent you want to be. When we take the pressure off ourselves, we free up energy that can help us to get to know our children in a more meaningful way and allow them to know us.

I know many women who are so caught up with all they do for their children—the daily activities, chauffeuring, providing clothes and meals—that they leave themselves little time to play a game or enjoy an activity with their child. Many are so intent on giving their children the best of everything, they seldom take the time to have a conversation, to really listen to their children's concerns or what they think about. When we listen, we can discover the unique and special individuals our children are and how they may be different from us.

Pam said, "I remembered being bored to tears on long Sunday afternoons as a child. Since Robin was an only child like me, I made a special effort to have her playmates over on Sundays or to get together with other families. One day when I asked her who she would like to have over, she said, 'No one! I want to play by myself.' I was floored. It was the first time I realized that all this planning was my idea.

"Since then I've come to realize she's not the social child I was. Sundays are her time-alone days where she can build her long and elaborate stories about her dolls. She sees enough children all week long. I'm proud that she has this other side. I try to honor it. It taught me to trust Robin to make more of the decisions about her activities and what she needs."

Giving of Ourselves

Another important part of mothering is the willingness to share yourself, who you are and your own journey. I encourage parents to talk with their children, person to person, not only adult to child or mother to son. Share your opinions and how you came to these conclusions, reflect on where you are now in your life and how you feel about it. This does not mean that you share information about your childhood that your children will not understand or that will frighten them. If you're an incest survivor, you will not tell your six-year-old daughter of your experience. But you can allow your children to know you and know what in general terms helped you to develop your resilience.

Don't feel you need to shield your child from everyday reality. Children need to learn that life doesn't always go the way we want. When something disappoints or frustrates you, you can share that information appropriately. Demonstrate the problem solving that life entails and how alternatives are found. When you have completed a project that has a special meaning for you, let your children know the sense of accomplishment you feel. The more resilience you model, the more your children will be able to develop their own.

Mothering and Work

Perhaps one of the hardest decisions mothers face today is deciding whether and how much to work outside the home. The debate continues among professionals and nonprofessionals alike on the effect of a mother's absence on her children. I believe what is best for one family will not be the same for another. It is a question of individual need, both for the parents and the child.

Shauna felt that she was lucky not to have to work. She said, "Al and I decided that once we began to have children, my place was home with them. I agreed to this, but now that I'm a mom, I'm not sure that it is enough for me. I'm bored. I love being with my baby, but it ties me down. I miss the challenge of my old job and the chance to get out and be with other adults."

Staying at home after a baby is born can be isolating for some women. They need and crave more stimulation. Shauna used her inner voice and took a realistic appraisal of who she was and what she needed to recommit to her role as mother. Realizing what she needed to feel fulfilled meant she could explore other options, rather than just feel resentful of her isolation and perhaps direct this resentment against her son.

If you work outside the home, as more than 60 percent of women with children under eighteen do, the demands of child care heaped upon the responsibilities of work and home may leave you little personal time. This can be a trial for many women, who often feel anger and frustration with themselves that they cannot somehow keep it all together. Again, much of what affects women here is the expectation that they should be able to follow their family traditions of child care, merely adding the job onto this. The stress level from this approach is high and can lead to a dissatisfaction with themselves, their work, and their children.

More and more women are choosing to have their children later in life, after establishing a career. For them, the needs of a child may conflict more directly with their career direction. It is one thing to want a child, but quite another to reconcile the time and energy required to care for a child or two with a career that involves emotional commitment, long hours, travel, and high job stress.

Many women in this position feel torn. They want to be with their children, but cannot spend as much time with them as they'd like. They also don't want to lose momentum in their career, in which they also have an investment.

Whatever your situation, take time to listen to the signals of what works best for you and your family. Listen also for signals that your life is out of balance and new solutions are needed.

What I Expect From Myself as a Mother

You may want to give yourself time to think about this exercise before you commit your answers to paper. Go through your day and allow your resilient voice to notice and to comment upon what you do well and what you may be taking for granted. Allow yourself to be clear about what frustrates you. When you are ready, answer these questions:

- How do you expect you will treat your children?
- How do you feel you should provide for your children? List all the things you feel you should be able to do for them in one day.
- How do you feel that you should provide for your home? List all the things that you feel you should be able to do on a daily basis and on a weekly basis.
- How do you feel you should be able to take care of yourself? List again what you should be able to do for yourself daily and weekly.
- How do you feel you should be able to take care of your marriage or other significant relationship? Again list what you should be able to do daily and weekly.
- In your answers, have you made any allowance for your being rushed, tired, ill, distracted, or upset? That is, are you assuming optimum conditions, or have you made concessions to the reality of everyday life?
- When things don't go as you planned, what do you expect from yourself? Do you treat yourself with the same tenderness you give to your children, or are you hard and critical on yourself? Do you model patience and forgiveness for yourself when you make a mistake, or are you too demanding of yourself?

The Effect of Children on Mothers

Many women are surprised to discover that their priorities and values shift as they become parents. What was fine before is no longer acceptable, or the high standards of housekeeping they had maintained now seem simply absurd. Often motherhood is seen as a time to get serious, to settle down, and to make some long-delayed changes.

Cristina had always wanted to move away from the dirt and crime of her native Los Angeles. She said, "I felt growing up in the city was too hard. I know, because I did it. As a young adult, newly on my own, I liked being close to my family, not far from old high school friends. But after Junior was born, I realized that I didn't want him to have to develop the street smarts that I did and so we moved."

Sometimes the identity changes are profound. Laura grew up on a reservation. "I loved being involved in tribal activities, especially dancing," said Laura. "I felt especially proud of my heritage at these times. But when I started to go off the reservation to go to school, I felt such shame at the racial slurs I received. I was torn being a bi-cultural Creek and so confused about why I was even alive. Most of my family had been killed through the years, from the forced marches of my grandmother's generation that killed so many of us, to the suicide and addiction in my generation. It was hard to reconcile why I had been chosen to live. So when I met Willie and fell in love, the idea of having a child frightened me. But then we had Thomas. Being a mother made it much easier to make peace with my own racial and cultural identity. I feel now that I know why I am alive. It is to carry the story of my people's struggle and resilience to the next seven generations."

How Parenting Kindles Childhood Memories

There are scores of books on the market about child rearing and how to parent, yet the primary basis of our concept of how to mother comes from the traditions of the family we grew up in. If we are fortunate, we have received a strong set of values from which to draw. Even if we choose not to follow particular practices, having a sense of tradition gives us an essential confidence we need to counterbalance our inevitable low moments. These traditions give us a head start in determining how we will show love to our child, set limits, and express anger, as well as how we deal with diaper rash, sibling rivalry, and tantrums.

But a mother who comes from a home environment that she feels she must reject will have a very different approach to mothering. She especially must use her resilience. The very process of parenting will give her ample opportunities to grow as she confronts the trials of the moment and recalls her own childhood challenges.

Being a parent is a rich experience for it draws upon not just skills acquired as an adult, but also our own memories of being a child. As a mother we need to make some important decisions that will immediately bring us back to what we experienced as a child. Do we allow our baby to cry herself to sleep at night or do we go in to comfort her? Do we get the milk our toddler asks for or do we teach him to get it for himself? Do we drive our teenagers where they need to go or do we let them know the times we are available and have them determine their commitments accordingly?

Each of these decisions, as well as countless more, evokes our own childhood. As we work with our children about their need for independence with their need for comfort and nurturance, we are transported back to the times when we struggled in the same way. Through recognition of these memories, we achieve the capacity to resolve them for ourselves.

For a woman with balanced resilience this is a bittersweet experience. Happy and sad memories are mixed, stimulated by the present activities of their own children. As these memories are recalled, she may use them to determine her actions, remembering what she appreciated most from her mother or other caretakers and offering what she chooses from these.

Women who have developed other resilience patterns as a result of a difficult childhood must also deal with memories of the trauma and will find parenting more difficult. The emotionally charged memories recalled may still be unresolved, drawing energy away from their interactions with their child. These memories may also evoke strong feelings that intensify the interactions. In fact, this is one way of determining that a memory or belief from our own childhood is present. Our interactions with our children will seem much more intense than they should. We may even hear our resilient voice saying, *Hey, what's going on here?* as we spin out of control. Recognizing when our reactions are out of proportion to the situation can be a good indication that we need to ask ourselves about the origins of the reaction.

Some parents are traumatized by their own impulses toward their children. They are racked with guilt. When they lose control and scream or hit their children, they feel that they can never forgive themselves. Parenting for them is like a large pit that they dig deeper with each interaction they wished they had handled differently.

No parent wants to scream at a child, and no child wants to be screamed at, but this does happen. It is these moments that bring back our own childhood to us. If there is pain lurking there, it will be remembered.

"I know what it is like to be hit as a child," abuse survivors lament. "I vowed I would never hurt my child. Here I am out of control just like my parents!"

All women caught in such pain need to begin looking at the context in which they have caused their children distress. When a woman comes to me in this kind of pain, I ask her first how the incident started. Was she aware when she began to lose control? What did she do afterward?

Chelsea was such a woman. She had married for the second time had one child and a second on the way. She was concerned that she was screaming too much at her seven-year-old son. When I asked her about her own childhood, she told me that she was never hit as a child, but she would be yelled at when her father would beat her mother, sometimes violently enough for her mother to be sent to the hospital. Chelsea sobbed and said, "I'm just like my father."

She would feel such remorse at her behavior that she would withdraw from her son. Later she would hope that he had forgotten it. I encouraged her to speak to him about her behavior, to explain that she was wrong and felt sorry for her actions. I told her she should be prepared to listen if he brought up a story from the past where she was wrong and to acknowledge his pain by saying, "I know that was tough for you."

What Chelsea and all parents need to understand is the vast difference between the first instance, when the child's pain is not responded to, and the second, when the child's distress is seen and addressed. In the first instance, the child must try to figure out what has happened. Alone and confused, a child will need to make some assumptions regarding what has happened. Rather than blame a parent and risk feeling that there is no one who can take care of her, she may choose to blame herself. This is the unconscious fear that many parents who have experienced trauma have—that their child will blame herself and learn to take on responsibility for everything, just as they learned to do.

In the second situation, however, the adult explains to the child and demonstrates how people accept responsibility and make amends. While this may look like the same experience, it is dramatically different for the child. Here the child's upset is acknowledged and validated. The child comes to understand limits of acceptable behavior, even when it is the parent and not herself who is at fault.

"Your yelling at your son is not the same as your father's yelling at you. You may even be using your father's words," I assured Chelsea, "but the experience for your child is different."

Chelsea began to understand that she was not like her father, that it was not just the words and tone that hurt her as a child, but the overall feelings surrounding these incidents. What happened before her outbursts of temper and what happened after were completely different than what she had experienced as a child. They, more than the outburst, determined the effect of the incident on her son.

With less remorse and anxiety about her actions, Chelsea began to look at what she needed to do to reduce her stress level and not lose control in the first place. She felt better about herself and her child, and this carried over into their other interactions. This, too, increased her sense of control.

Please note: If you find yourself out of control, hitting or otherwise abusing your child, seek professional help to protect your child. Even spanking can be physically abusive and damaging. At best, it teaches that violence is an acceptable means of problem solving. At worst, it can endanger the health and safety of your child.

Evaluating Our Past

Knowing that we will find ourselves doing most naturally what we ourselves experienced as a child encourages us to consider the past in the hopes of discovering the best of what we received, so that we can make use of it in the present. It also gives us the chance to change what we need. To do this we need to understand the parenting we received so we can better visualize the parent that we want to be.

Give yourself a couple of minutes to relax and think back to your own childhood. Allow your resilient voice to answer for you:

- What did you like most about the parenting you received?
- What made you feel most secure as a child?
- What is one of your most happy memories as a child?
- What is one of your saddest memories as a child?
- How did you think you would parent your children when you grew up?
- How do you feel you are doing as a parent now?

Remembering our own childhood can allow us to notice when the child that we were in the past is present and needing to be remembered. It can allow us to enjoy the experiences of our own child as we reexperience the wonder and joy of discovery that characterizes this time in our life.

Healing the Past

It is natural in situations like Chelsea's to want to isolate these painful incidents and pretend that they do not matter. Similarly, when strong memories from our own childhood are triggered, especially if we are not quite conscious of what is affecting us this way, we may want to push them aside, lock them up, and avoid them. Over time, however, this can lead to our feeling increasingly out of control, overwhelmed, and guilty—all of which will serve to make us less effective and to diminish the enjoyment we receive from motherhood.

Instead of shoving them away, we can use these moments to recognize what unresolved issues we have and thereby heal the memories of the past. We can also better understand how we survived by developing our resilience. Over time, our efforts at understanding also serve to diminish the intensity of these moments. The more we recognize the unresolved part of us that seeks expression, the less it will need to gain our attention through such interactions as those with our children.

Becky was a young mother who consulted me about her fear that she was an abusive parent to her eighteen-month-old daughter. Becky herself had been abused as a child. She came from an alcoholic home in which physical violence between adults, and adults and children, was a norm. She pledged she'd never to do the same to her child, yet was fearful that she was. She was full of shame.

When we met, she spoke of having very intense feelings of rage towards her daughter, even though she deeply loved her. After I determined that she was not impulsive in nature and therefore unlikely to act out these feelings, I encouraged her to connect with the thought or memory that was behind her transition from anger at her daughter to rage.

One day she came in smiling. "I got it!" she said. She then related that the day before her daughter was on the other side of her king-size bed. "I saw her walking toward my jewelry box. I felt the anger rising, but I thought, What is this? What is going on? I dropped down into the part of me that was so very, very angry. I remembered that when I was a child no one ever respected my belongings. I suddenly felt sad for the little girl that was me. I could feel that this was the source of my anger, not my daughter's actions. I felt such joy and relief at this discovery. I know this never would have come if I didn't trust myself enough to delve into what I was feeling."

By working through the feeling and connecting to this memory, Becky's anger toward her daughter began to be less intense and occur less frequently. Becky realized she would always be somewhat sensitive about her personal belongings. She used this realization to set limits on her daughter's access to her most valued possessions. Becky also found that by her simple acknowledgment of its importance to her, the issue began to resolve itself.

In this and other ways, Becky recognized a pattern in the situations that caused her anger, which enabled her to avoid them, or to control her anger when confronted with them. This is an option we have as parents—to get to know the part in us that is again experiencing our own childhood through the activities of our child and to use this knowledge in our parenting and in other areas of life.

As we become more aware of the issues that evoke our deepest responses, we gain mastery over them, and they lose their ability to move us in the same way. Even the past can lose its hold over us, if we choose to bring our resilience to bear upon it.

Changing Our Legacies

We often think of the traditions of our childhood as cast in stone, but they are not. As we realize the range and nature of choices we can make as parents, we can begin to set our priorities in all areas of our family's life. This means selecting rituals and celebrations that have meaning for us, regardless of past associations.

Rituals, such as birthday parties, family holidays, and community events, take on their importance through their relevance to our lives and our need to celebrate their meanings. Here we can use our inner voice to decide what remains meaningful and what we want to change from the ways of the past.

Joanne, a member of Al-Anon, a self-help organization for those who have been affected by someone else's drinking, decided that she no longer needed to serve alcoholic beverages at family gatherings. She wanted her children to see people enjoying themselves sober. So she changed the rules and changed the types of memories her children will have of the whole family together.

Lois, a working single mother, wanted to make birthdays special, even when the demands of work and school meant that she and her children spent most of the day apart. The night before, Joanne would blow up balloons to tie around her children's room as they slept. In the morning they awakened to a bright and cheerful room.

The stories we tell are also important rituals. We can choose to foster our children's understanding of themselves and the world around them by developing and telling family stories that emphasize resilience. This can be a formidable contribution to their lives.

Lisa realized that she came from a family in which women always saw themselves as victims and competed with each other to see who had the worst of it.

"I was always angry at these tales, even as a kid," said Lisa. "With my daughters I now emphasize how the women in our family persevered over great obstacles, how they kept the family together through the immigration from South America, how they survived the Great Depression and abusive husbands, and how they learned to become businesspeople in America. There were some really outstanding women—and I'm proud to tell my daughters of them."

Breaking the Rules

Perhaps the most important realization a mother can make is that she has power over her life and power over the quality of life she provides for her children. When we make our expectations and our own experiences conscious, we can view them against the reality of our everyday lives to see what fits and what doesn't.

Gloria was an executive secretary. She said, "I love my work, which is lucky since I need to work to keep up with the mortgage payments. I have the world's best boss. But every night I'd go home and feel like the world's worst mother. It took some time before I realized that I had to shift some of my expectations of myself. I couldn't work, keep up with the house, and serve a well-balanced meal each night. But I did try, for a while. Daughter number two did me in.

"So, after many arguments with myself regarding how children are supposed to be raised, and what my mother and my mother-in-law did, I realized that for my sanity we would have to do it differently. Dinner at my home may be a bowl of cereal or a sandwich, and there are dust balls on the floor. But we are all much happier. I have time to play with my girls and time to relax a little. All it took was listening to myself and changing the rules."

We often forget that as parents we are the ones who make the rules, and who can break the rules when we need to. When we set our priority to be a good mother and listen to our resilient voice, we can find the means to do it. We can identify the changes we need to make to bring greater satisfaction into our parenting.

As we look back over our lives, we may be surprised at the varied designs we see there, much like a patchwork quilt of many colors and textures that form an overall pattern which may not be easy at first to discern. Whether this perspective comes earlier in our lives, or later, it reveals that we are far more complex than we first thought. We each have a richness, a depth that is ours alone.

We derive this depth from our many experiences, large and small, for we are the product of many influences. We are the child who heard stories of grandmother's clever ways of surviving the Depression by making dresses of sack cloth from bags of grain. We are the girl who worried about being attractive and desirable. We are the angry woman who found the courage to stand up for herself and what she knows is right. Perhaps we are the wounded woman who has known rape, or the young woman who survived incest, racial discrimination, or the early death of a parent. We are the tired woman who struggled to maintain a home and provide for her family. We are the aging woman in a society that places little value on the elderly. We are all that we have been, are now, and will be.

The unifying element within us, the aspect that can help us understand all these various selves and how they merge to comprise all of who we are, is our resilience. It reflects our own special blend of facets, developed and fine-tuned by the stresses and adversity we have faced.

Our resilience begins to gather within us from our earliest childhood experiences and continues to grow into our golden years. It brings to bear the best of our roots and provides us the vision of our wings.

Once recognized, our resilience forms a blueprint for organizing the strengths and insights we can rely on in times of tension, crises, disappointments, and trauma. We can draw on it also to see us through the demands of everyday life. Whether this involves the juggling of family and employment, the challenge of aging, or the charting of new directions, each of us has within her a capacity to persevere despite obstacles.

As we integrate these strengths into our lives, we can begin also to address larger issues, such as our overall personal development, major life changes, and our search for spiritual meaning.

Listening

As we have seen, our resilience is an inner presence that speaks to us, whether we hear, feel, or envision its counsel. If we permit it, this presence can inform and shape our actions and responses.

With practice we can learn to use this facility on a daily basis, discovering that we may very well have more answers than we think. Learning to listen is crucial to developing our resilience in a more conscious manner. Here are four easy guidelines for developing your resilient voice.

1. *Listen to your resilient voice.* Learn to distinguish this voice from all the other voices you have internalized. Focus on hearing this particular voice, as it is the one that speaks for you.

2. *Speak with your resilience.* Develop the ability to have a dialogue with this part of who you are, whether by daydreaming, meditating, visualizing, or journal writing. Remember, there is no right way; the best way is the one that works for you.

3. *Make a commitment to access your resilient voice.* Make time on a daily basis to communicate with this important part of you. Get in the habit of using this inner resource when you need to decide what is right for you.

4. *Integrate your resilience into your life.* Find opportunities to use your resilience in your decision making, in your reflections on what you've done or on an action you would like to take. Using your resilience can make sure that you take time to do things for yourself.

Once you have identified your resilience, learned to hear its counsel, and use it regularly to make decisions in your life, it becomes a conscious part of your personality and an added dimension of who you are. In this way, you can use your resilience to live your life in such a way that you can positively influence those around you, your children, your friends, even society. This influence can be beneficial and lasting.

Resilience in Our Lives

After you have begun to work on a daily basis with your resilience, ask yourself the following questions:

- Is your resilient voice becoming a clearer presence within you?
- In what ways do you find that you are more aware of your resilience?
- Do you find yourself consciously using your resilience to assist you?
- Do you find yourself more confident?
- Are you seeing positive changes in your life?
- Are you beginning to see less costly ways of protecting yourself?
- Are you beginning to feel you can take risks to get more of your needs met?
- Are you finding that you are more willing to risk being awkward in areas that you are less sure in?
- Are you more comfortable with your dark side?
- Are you beginning to sense your own inner power?
- Are you beginning to exercise your personal power?
- Are you finding it easier to make decisions?
- Do you feel that you are beginning to spread your wings?

A yes to even a few of these questions is a clear indication that you are successfully utilizing your resilience.

Personal Balance and Development

Our resilience is shaped and molded by the myriad influences in our lives that may have caused an imbalance or a lack of development. If you have begun to work with your resilience to enhance your personal development, you may find that your original pattern of resilience has changed.

Ask yourself the following questions beginning with the resilience style that most described you initially.

Balanced Resilience

- Are you more conscious of your own power?
- Do you sense your resilience?
- Do you find yourself using your resilience in difficult moments?
- Do you feel that you have access to more of who you are?

Undeveloped Resilience

- Are you beginning to see that you can make decisions about what is right for you?
- Do you find yourself now having more opinions concerning issues that involve you?
- Do you feel excited as you begin to stretch your wings?
- Are you developing a vision of the future that takes into account more of your needs and your growing ability to achieve them?

Paradoxical Resilience

- Are you using your skills in more than one area?
- Are you beginning to see choices you can make in the areas of your life where you have exercised less power previously?
- Do you feel more whole and less like two different people?
- Are you more confident, taking risks in areas in which you are less developed?

Self-Contained Resilience

- Are you finding that you desire to be with others more?
- Are you beginning to take risks outside your main area of competence?
- Are you finding that your identity is broadening and no longer tied to just one domain?

- Are you beginning to bring others into your life?

Overwhelmed Resilience

- Are you relaxing more, realizing that the worst struggles are over and you have made it through them?
- Are you beginning to feel that you have choices to make?
- Are you finding that you are being less hard on yourself?
- Are you finding that there is more to like in you?

Stellar Resilience

- Do you find you are letting others take care of you rather than trying to be the primary caretaker all of the time?
- Have you been able to slow down a little and smell the roses?
- Do you feel more sure of yourself and that your successes are less a factor of luck than the result of your own initiative?
- Do you sense that you are beginning to achieve a more comfortable balance in your life?

It may be that you find a dramatic shift in your resilience pattern or a gradual change. There is no wrong way. When we speak about developing resilience we are speaking more of a general direction rather than a specific destination, so any change is significant. The important question is, Do you see a different pattern emerging? If so, you are on your way to developing your greater potential.

Transforming Our Lives

In addition to helping us deal with daily demands and our personal development, our resilience can assist us in determining the nature and direction of significant changes needed in our lives. This is because our resilience contains an invaluable amount of information and the wisdom to show us how to use this information in the satisfaction of our needs.

As you go through your days, notice areas of frustration, disappointment, or emptiness. These small, vague feelings over time indicate that something in our lives isn't working as it should. Whether it's a relationship, a job, or a lifestyle issue, such as alcohol use or money management, the constant friction that results can wear us down and sap our strength. Use your resilience to name the source of this problem.

Think about an area of your life you would like to change. Ask your resilient voice to help you answer the following questions:

1. What area would you like to change in your life?
   - What is this situation now?
   - What will it look like when it is changed? Be specific.
2. What are the first three steps to help you make this change?
3. What resources do you need to make this change?
4. How long will it take?
5. When can you begin?

In this way, we can bring about the changes we need to live the life we want. We can take care of ourselves, allow others into our lives, have control, and use our power.

Meaning in Our Lives

An essential element of our lives is the personal journey toward spiritual meaning. Here we look for symbols that connect us to a greater sphere of wisdom that we can use to claim all of who we are. We search for symbols outside of ourselves to reinforce what we have within.

For many women, the search for identity and meaning has led them toward traditional sources of spirituality and wisdom. They find great value in Christian, Judaic, Islamic, Eastern, or Native American practices. Other women's searches have led them to an appreciation of the feminine strength found in the Great Mother archetype. Here is a source of adaptability and wisdom that harkens back to the beginning of time.

History shows that the first deities were female. The earliest religions worshipped the Great Mother, rather than God the Father. In religions such as Hinduism, we find goddesses such as Shakti and Kali. Many Native American cultures worship Mother Earth. History is full of allusions to women's wisdom, power, and sagacity.

The Goddess possesses two aspects, a duality of light and dark, which maintain a perfect balance. The light side of the Goddess is the nurturer, the giver of life, the giver of crops, the source of rain and reproduction; life itself is her domain. The dark side of the Goddess is the devourer, the taker of life: the destroyer of what she has sown. This side was represented in early religions as the source of famine, pestilence, death. This is the part of the Goddess that must be appeased or devastation will lie in her wake. This image of the Goddess acknowledges our own natural cycles of light and dark, joy and loss, life and death.

These symbols echo with our own inner experience and are very much in keeping with traditionally feminine beliefs about the natural cycle of life. As we face an unending series of challenges, we take heart from knowing this, expecting this, and making room for it. In knowing more about the earliest religions, when women were the deities, we may find a greater richness and depth. We find roots and a respected place beyond our personal history that our larger society does not often afford today. We receive an affirmation of who we are in total—our light as well as dark side—that leads us to overcome shame and claim power.

Taking Our Resilience Forward

Our resilience is the part of us that celebrates cycles: it looks forward to new beginnings and back to past lessons. Our resilience is our ally in times of hardship and loss. Whether we lose our youth, a once valued relationship, a job, a loved one, or our home, losses are an inevitable and natural part of the life cycle. Our resilience can give us permission to grieve and resolve these losses. In the midst of our sorrow, it remembers the promise of rebirth, and brings to us the strength we have developed through past struggles.

We begin life learning, we end it knowing. In using this knowing on our own behalf, we enrich our lives and enhance the future. It is our resilience that allows us to benefit from this knowing, to look into the future with a new understanding of what lies ahead. As we age, we gather our accumulated wisdom to light the way, to make sense of all of the new experiences that are before us, and to allow us to understand and make peace with the past.

Our resilience is the part of ourselves that is steadfast amid change, an inner compass that charts our way. Listening to it, we can have faith in it and rely on it.

Adler, T. "Bad Mix: Combat Stress, Decisions." *The APA Monitor* 24: 3 (1993).

Anderson, S. R., and P. Hopkins. *The Feminine Face of God: The Unfolding of the Sacred in Women.* New York: Bantam Books, 1991.

Anthony, J., and B. Cohler, eds. *The Invulnerable Child.* New York: Guilford Press, 1987.

Anthony, J., and C. Koupernik, eds. *The Child in His Family: Children at Psychiatric Risk.* New York: John Wiley and Sons, 1974.

Bennett, L., and S. Wolin. "Family Identity, Ritual and Myth: A Cultural Perspective on Life Cycle Transitions." In *Family Transitions: Continuity and Change over the Life Cycle,* edited by C. Falicov, 211-234. New York: Guilford Press, 1988.

Bennett, L., S. Wolin, D. Reiss, and M. Teitelbaum. "Couples at Risk for Transmission of Alcoholism: Protective Influences." *Family Process* 26 (1987): 111-129.

Bettleheim, B. "The Modern Family . . . The Impact on Its Children." Keynote Address at the National Association on Children of Alcoholics Annual Conference, February 1987.

Bolen, J. S. *Goddesses in Everywoman: A New Psychology of Women.* New York: Harper Colophon, 1985.

Boundy, D. *When Money is the Drug: The Compulsion for Credit, Cash and Chronic Debt.* San Francisco: HarperSanFrancisco, 1993.

Bowen, M. "A Family System Approach to Alcoholism." *Addiction* 21 (1974).

Brown, M. L., and C. Gilligan. *Meeting at the Crossroads: Women's Psychology and Girls' Development.* New York: Ballantine, 1992.

Brownmiller, S. *Against Our Will: Men, Women, and Rape.* New York: Bantam Books, 1981.

Carlson, K. *In Her Image: The Unhealed Daughter's Search for Her Mother.* Boston: Shambhala, 1989.

Chodorow, N. *The Reproduction of Mothering: Psychoanalysis and the Sociology of Gender.* Berkeley: University of California Press, 1978.

Curran, D. *Traits of a Healthy Family.* New York: Ballantine, 1984.

Debold, E., M. Wilson, and I. Malave. *Mother-Daughter Revolution, From Betrayal to Power.* New York: Addison-Wesley, 1993.

De Lange, J. "Depression in Women: Explanations and Prevention." In *Women, Power, and Change,* edited by A. Weick and S. Vandiver.

Washington, D.C.: National Association of Social Workers, 1980.

Dobson, J. *Love Must Be Tough: New Hope for Families in Crises.* Waco, Texas: Word Books, 1983.

———. *What Wives Wish Their Husbands Knew About Women.* Wheaton, Ill.: Tyndale House Publishers, 1975.

Dowling, C. *The Cinderella Complex: Woman's Hidden Fear of Independence.* New York: Pocket Books, 1981.

Elder, D. *Women of the Bible Speak to Women of Today.* Marina del Rey, California: DeVorss & Co., 1986.

Ehrenreich, B., and D. English. "Blowing the Whistle on the 'Mommy Track.'" *Ms.* 18 (1989): 56-63.

———. *For Her Own Good: 150 Years of the Experts' Advice to Women.* New York: Anchor/Doubleday, 1978.

Estès, C. P. *Women Who Run with the Wolves: Myths and Stories of the Wild Woman Archetype.* New York: Ballantine, 1992.

Faludi, S. *Backlash: The Undeclared War Against American Women.* New York: Doubleday, 1991.

Felsman, J. K. "Risk and Resiliency in Childhood: The Lives of Street Children." In *The Child in Our Times: Studies in the Development of Resiliency,* edited by T. Dugan and R. Coles, 59-80. New York: Brunner/Mazel, 1989.

Freilberg, P. "Self-Esteem Gender Gap Widens In Adolescence." *APA Monitor* 22: 4 (1991): 29.

French, M. *The War Against Women.* New York: Summit Books, 1992.

Fromm, E. *The Art of Loving.* New York: Basic Books, 1963.

Garber, J., and M. E. D. Seligman, eds. *Human Helplessness: Theory and Application.* New York: Academic Press, 1980.

Gilligan, C. *In a Different Voice: Psychological Theory and Women's Development.* Cambridge, Mass.: Harvard University Press, 1983.

Gilligan, C., P. L. Lyons, and T. J. Hanmer. *Making Connections: The Relational World of Adolescent Girls at Emma Willard School.* Cambridge, Mass.: Harvard University Press, 1990.

Hochschild, A. *The Second Shift.* New York: Avon Books, 1989.

Hirschmann, J., and C. Hunter. *Overcoming Overeating.* New York: Fawcett Columbine, 1989.

Jack, D. C. *Silencing the Self: Women and Depression.* Cambridge, Mass.: Harvard University Press, 1991.

Johnson, M. *Strong Mothers, Weak Wives: The Search for Gender Equality.* Berkeley: University of California, 1988.

Kagan, J. *The Nature of the Child.* New York: Basic Books, 1984.

Kersey, K., ed. *Helping Your Child Handle Stress.* Washington, D.C.: Acropolis Books, 1986.

Marks, J. *Hidden Children: The Secret Survivors of the Holocaust.* New York: Ballantine, 1993.

Miller, A. *The Drama of the Gifted Child.* New York: Basic Books, 1981.

Miller, J. B. *Toward a New Psychology of Women.* Boston: Beacon Press, 1976.

Mussen, P. H., J. J. Conger, and J. Kagan. *Child Development and Personality,* 3d ed. New York: Harper & Row, 1969.

O'Gorman, P. "Codependency and Women: Unraveling the Power Behind Learned Helplessness." In *Feminist Perspectives on Addictions,* edited by N. Van Den Bergh. New York: Springer Publishing, 1992.

————. "Codependency Explored: A Social Movement in Search of Definition and Treatment." *Psychiatric Quarterly* 64 (Summer 1993): 199-212.

————. "Developmental Aspects of Codependency." *Counselor Magazine* (March-April 1990): 14-16.

————. "Self-Concept, Locus of Control and Perception of Father in Adolescents from Homes With and Without Severe Drinking Problems." Ph.D. diss., Fordham University, 1976.

————. *Self-Parenting Twelve-Step Workbook: Windows to Your Inner Child.* Deerfield Beach, Fla.: Health Communications, 1990.

————. "Teaching Parenting Skills." *Counselor Magazine* (January-February 1990): 20-21.

O'Gorman, P., and P. Oliver-Diaz. *Breaking the Cycle of Addiction: A Parent's Guide to Raising Healthy Kids.* Deerfield Beach, Fla.: Health Communications, 1987.

Oliver-Diaz, P., and P. O'Gorman. *Twelve Steps to Self-Parenting for Adult Children of Alcoholics.* Deerfield Beach, Fla.: Health Communications, 1988.

Papp, P. *The Process of Change.* New York: The Guildford Press, 1983.

Schwartz, F. "Management Women and the New Facts of Life." *Harvard Business Review* (January-February 1989): 67-74.

Seligman, M. E. P. *Helplessness: On Depression, Development and Death.* San Francisco: Freeman, 1974.

————. *Learned Optimism: How to Change Your Mind and Your Life.* Edited by Julie Rubenstein. New York: Pocket Books, 1992.

Sheehy, G. "The Flaming Fifties." *Vanity Fair* 56 (October 1993).

Steinem, G. *Revolution from Within: A Book of Self-Esteem.* Boston: Little, Brown and Company, 1992.

Steinglass, P., et al. *The Alcoholic Family.* New York: Basic Books, 1987.

Tannen, D. *You Just Don't Understand.* New York: Ballantine, 1990.

Werner, E., and R. Smith. *Vulnerable but Invincible: A Longitudinal Study of Resilient Children and Youth.* New York: Adams, Bannister, Cox, 1992.

———. *Overcoming the Odds: High Risk Children from Birth to Adulthood.* Ithaca: Cornell University Press, 1992.

Whipple, B., and G. Ogden. *Safe Encounters: How Women Can Say "Yes" to Pleasure and "No" to Unsafe Sex.* McGraw-Hill: New York, 1989.

Wolin, S. and S. Wolin. *The Resilient Self: How Survivors of Troubled Families Rise Above Adversity.* New York: Random House, 1993.

Patricia O'Gorman, Ph.D., is a cofounder of the National Association for Children of Alcoholics and founding director of the Department of Prevention and Education of the National Council on Alcoholism. She was a faculty member of the New York University School of Medicine, Department of Psychiatry. She is a nationally known lecturer and the coauthor of *Teaching About Alcohol, Breaking the Cycle of Addiction, Twelve Steps to Self-Parenting for Adult Children of Alcoholics,* and *Self-Parenting Twelve-Step Workbook: Windows to Your Inner Child.*

More titles of interest . . .

A Life of My Own
Meditations on Hope and Acceptance
> *by the author of* Each Day a New Beginning

A Life of My Own is the essential meditative guide for those looking for strength, serenity, and insight in their relationships with chemically dependent family members, coworkers, or friends. Includes reflections on faith, confidentiality and anonymity, attitudes, control, and trust that can help readers live more balanced lives. 400 pp.
Order No. 1070

Growing Whole
Self-Realization on an Endangered Planet
> *by Molly Young Brown*

Growing Whole offers readers a step-by-step guide to a profoundly revolutionary yet simple method of effecting change that bridges the gap between personal and global transformation. Molly Young Brown explains how to liberate one's natural ability to grow, learn, and act in harmony with others and the planet. 256 pp.
Order No. 5182

Finding Balance and Creativity
> *by Helene Lerner-Robbins*

These two books provide inspiring meditations that enhance spiritual development. *Finding Balance* helps readers learn to trust their unique process of personal and spiritual growth as a central road to serenity. *Creativity* adds to life the color and vitality that may be missing, and fills the seemingly mundane with joyous meaning. 96 pp. each.
Order No. 1493   *Finding Balance*
Order No. 1492   *Creativity*

For price and order information, or a free catalog, please call our
Telephone Representatives.
HAZELDEN EDUCATIONAL MATERIALS

1-800-328-9000   **1-612-257-4010**   **1-612-257-1331**
(Toll-Free, U.S., Canada   *(Outside the U.S. & Canada)*   *(FAX)*
& the Virgin Islands)

Pleasant Valley Road • P.O. Box 176 • Center City, MN 55012-0176